FOODIE
TRAVEL

adventures in eating & drinking
+ food, cooking & fun guides

NEAR & FAR

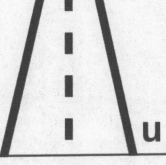

C. R. Luteran

I'm most thankful for the gift of sight which has allowed me to see the world and what I'm eating.

Unfortunately, not all people have food to eat, so I will be using some of the proceeds from the sale of this book, to help in the fight against hunger through donations to the following organizations:

Feeding America
World Central Kitchen
City Harvest (NYC)
East Hampton Food Pantry (NY)
Food 1st Foundation (NYC)
Garces Foundation
Island Food Pantry (Martha's Vineyard, MA)
St. Francis of Assisi Kitchen (Scranton, PA)
The Trussell Trust (UK)
Welcome Table Soup Kitchen (NYC)

A donation will be made to the Alzheimer's Association in loving memory of my father.

u go near & far Tiny Press
First Paperback Edition.
Published in the USA & UK

A catalogue record of this book is available from the
British Library.

ISBN 978-1-7333161-0-1

Wholesale Orders & Foreign Rights:
sales@foodietravelnearandfaratravelbook.com

Book Readings & Physical/Virtual Events:
press@foodietravelnearandfaratravelbook.com

Say hello:
havefun@foodietravelnearandfaratravelbook.com

It took almost 30 years to write this book and to eat the world. The goal was to write a book about food & culture from a traveler's near & far experiences for others to enjoy and use as a guide.

I want to thank my family & friends for encouraging me to publish this book, however, possible. There were times when I almost gave up, but I kept on going like that little blue Sri Lankan train chugging up into the hilly green and misty fields dotted with tea plants.

I'm not a famous chef. I'm just someone who likes to eat and cook food. I cook by taste and never write my ad hoc recipes down, so I can kind of sort of make the same dish twice, but a little bit different each time. I'm an unknown writer, also, but a seasoned traveler. Of course, global events occurred in 2019/2020 which canceled or made attendance at major book fairs such as London, NY, or Frankfurt difficult or impossible, but where there's a will there's a way, even if it's not via the traditional method.

The Greek word, "meraki," made this book possible.

ENJOY!

Table of Contents

Dobrou chut´! Bon appétit! Guten Appetit!
Kalí órexi! Buon Appetito! Smacznego!
Desfrute de sua refeição! Smaklig spis!
Disfrute de su comida!
Enjoy your meal!

INTRODUCTION

Thank you for buying this book.

Look. Listen. Smell. Taste. Sip.

Come travel with me on these gastronomic journeys. If you're an armchair traveler, I hope they bring a place's cuisine home to your home.

Let these 100 bite-sized tasty vignettes and memoirs whet your appetites, tempt & satisfy your taste buds, excite, nourish, inspire, surprise, teach, and comfort you.

Get **"a sense of place"** and connect with people and places with each food & drink story.

Food and drink are a big part of life and create memories. Memories (happy or crazy) are the best souvenirs!

Open wide to avoid any food FOMO and let the adventure begin! Eat with your whole body. Let your eyes & mouth partake in sensory experiences.

How to Read This Book

Feel free to read this foodie book any way you want to. There is no right or wrong way. Perhaps on an empty stomach is best? Read it from beginning to end, by country, continent or skip around indulging in a rich and gooey chocolate tale or a curry cooking class in India.

Discover world flavors in your own neighborhood with the Food & Drink Guides.

Forage for yourself with the handy dandy Food & Drinks guides whether you're eating in, taking out, or getting a delivery. Perhaps cook up your own adventure with the DIY Cooking recommendations? Don't worry, you can bike or walk it all off using the Burning Calories section.

Let the Fun guide's book & movie section entertain you and transport you to other countries.

EATER BEWARE:

Places do come and go so please check open hours before venturing anywhere.

Dig In!

ASIA (SOUTH)

INDIA

New Delhi
A Dry Day

Really?!! A few days before a long-awaited dinner at The Spice Route at the Imperial Hotel; I received a rather confusing and disappointing e-mail from the restaurant. It stated that a dry day would be in effect that day. A dry day? The trip had been planned in the hope of only having dry days and no monsoon rain days. A dry day????

I broke the news to my mate who was a bit in disbelief until we verified it via some quick internet research. A dry day had absolutely nothing to do with the weather and everything to do with the upcoming election. No alcohol was available/served on a dry day. I would be lying if I said this news was not a big disappointment, so I will not. It was what it was. Disappointing! Any dreams of a cold and much needed Kingfisher or a chilled chardonnay after having endured a long flight with plain plane food would just have to be postponed.

After contemplating the situation for an hour or two, reality set in and we tried to look on the bright side. Perhaps dry days should be enforced worldwide during election season? Maybe then the right political leaders would be elected? There would be time for drinking later when winners could celebrate and losers could drown their sorrows in clear, yellow gold, amber, or red liquids.

A few days before the dry day news, I had to break other bad news. Air India had canceled our flight from New Delhi to Agra which meant that we'd have to take the train. We were time poor. At this point, I was afraid to read any more e-mails regarding the trip as I was starting to feel like a regular bearer of bad news. What a way to begin a trip before you'd even left home! Were we ever going to see the Taj Mahal, one of the New Seven Wonders of the World?

In any case, our flight to New Delhi touched down as scheduled in a city chock full of chaos, cows, and colors. Later that evening, we jumped into a cute Ambassador cab and made our way to the Spice Route. Our reservation was located as if it had been lost that would have been the third and last strike! The dining room was lovely with all its exotic, artsy, and colonial decorative touches. The South East Asian cuisine was infused with a mélange of spices that mesmerized your eyes and tantalized your taste buds. I went to sleep happy knowing that the next day would not be dry. Or dry but with alcohol! I slept well!
(February 2015)

New Delhi

A Cooking Class with Delhi Magic

Before leaving for India, I tried to book a cooking class with Delhi Magic (delhimagic.com) in Agra. The possibility of taking a local curry cooking class seemed like the "foodie" thing to do. Just the thought of it made me giddy with delight! Unfortunately, I received an e-mail reply saying that an Agra session was not possible. No. N O. No.

Not wanting to take "NO" for an answer as this might be my one & only trip to India; I sent another e-mail asking if we could do it in New Delhi. I received an e-mail saying "YES" it was possible. Being flexible and optimistic pays off in the end and sometimes the impossible is possible. Afterall, impossible really means, "I'm possible," right?

As instructed, we met our teacher/host, Neelima, near Green Park Station at 4:30 PM. I laughed a bit as I compared this Green Park to London's lovely and leafy Green Park near Buckingham Palace. We found each other easily enough based on her supplied description and on our looking like out-of-towners. She spoke English well enough, and we made small talk and discussed the itinerary as we walked. She led us to an outdoor market area where she carefully shopped for fruits and veggies such as okra, tomatoes, and onions. She stopped at a spice stall for some garam masala.

As we made our way through lively, hectic, and chaotic alleys, we marveled at the varied and continuously busy street trade economy. Welcome to life in India! Almost anything and everything can be bought on its streets. Fruit vendors constantly sprayed their edible wares with water to wash off any dust. All types of street foods from curries to nuts were cooked on crude stoves or rickety carts.

We passed a goat who wore a purse which made me crack up with laughter. Hopefully, not made from goat skin. What on earth were they shopping for? If only Anya Hindmarch could see this! I must tell her the next time we meet for lunch (which will be never) that she should make purses for goats. Afterall, she makes all kinds of kooky handbags like wrinkled crisps purses and cereal box purses.

After we procured ingredients for our cooking class, we walked about 20 minutes to our host's home. Upon our arrival, Neelima offered us a cup of Masala chai tea which we quickly accepted not fearing any issues since the water would be boiled. A few minutes later, she handed us cups of tea that smelled of ginger, herbs, and spices. Best tea ever! We quickly and appreciatively accepted a second cup. After chatting about life in India, the USA & UK for about a half hour it was time to get busy cooking!

Prior to our cooking lesson, I had received an e-mail saying that it would be a vegetarian cooking class. Neelima's kitchen was stocked with ingredients that you would except to see in any Indian home, curry house, or restaurant such as cardamom and coriander seeds, curry powder, turmeric powder, red chilli powder, cinnamon sticks, and basmati rice. Neelima took charge and we handed her ingredients as requested. She blended the vegetables for the curry sauces instead of dicing them which surprised us. We helped her stir colorful pots and chatted while we watched their contents gradually turn shades of orange, yellow, and red.

We cooked up Bhindi (Okra) Bhaji, Red Kidney Bean Curry, and Paneer Cheese. There were papadums, chutneys, and lime pickle to snack on, too.

The highlight of the cooking class was eating the meal that we had cooked with Neelima and her shy daughter in their dining room. Food is best when shared! She even gave us some leftovers to bring home. I mean to our home sweet hotel! *(February 2015)*

SRI LANKA (CEYLON)

Nuwara Eliya

A Tea Plantation, Tour & Tasting

The need to satisfy the curiosity about where my daily cup of tea (cuppa) comes from found me on a Sri Lankan train headed to Little England. Richly colored photos of the splendiferous tea country hills in travel magazines had seduced me, too. I wasn't in the market for buying a tea estate in Ceylon like Sir Thomas Lipton did in the late 1800's, but a love for tea made the visit a must "Go See Do" bucket list item.

Unfortunately, I had limited time here since I had made a last-minute trip to Malaysia where I ate some tasty nasi lemak and colorful ais kacang. But where there is a will, there is a way! After seeing some over the top ornate temples in Sri Lanka and Geoffrey Bawa's tropical modernism architecture in Colombo, it was time to head to Nuwara Eliya. I headed to the Colombo Fort Railway Station.

I would be slow traveling via train and bus. The entire day would be devoted to this tea quest. I had been on the road for a few weeks so was looking forward to the slower pace. The great thing about solo travel is the freedom to "carpe diem" when opportunities present themselves without having to double check with anyone. The worst thing about solo travel is that your mind and eyes are always on thinking about logistics and watching self & stuff. Bathroom visits and naps are easier to take when a buddy can be your eyes. I have taken many one-eye open naps over the years always feeling half-rested. Unfortunately, it's the price you pay for the freedom to do your own thing whenever and wherever!

To avoid any failures, disappointments, and FOMO, I purchased my ticket the day before. I was time poor now and there was no margin for error. The clock was quickly ticking! I went to window 17 where I easily bought a train ticket to Nanu Oya. The one-way 3rd class ticket cost 400 LKR (Sri Lankan Rupees) about 2 GBP. The trip from Colombo to Little England with a stop in Kandy would take around 6-1/2 hours. Very slow travel!

I enjoyed a curry and some hoppers (coconut and rice crepes) that night and went to bed early since I had to be on my way around daybreak.

Fortunately, I was able to get a bus ride to the train station at 5 AM unlike some places where public transportation started up a wee bit later. The train exceeded my expectations as it had windows that opened! I had been on some trains in India where that was not always the case. Of course, no interior amenities such as those found on a Eurostar or Amtrak train were expected. I was most grateful for their presence which made scenic views possible. They allowed me to stick my head out to see what was around the bend as the train climbed further up and into the hill country's curvy and mountainous landscape. Occasionally, I felt a cool au naturel mist on my face from the rain which was a bit more exotic than one from a canned facial spray. I cracked up laughing thinking about how this free wellness feature should be included and flaunted by Sri Lanka's Tourist Board in their ads to attract tourists.

Words and adjectives such as beautiful, breathtaking, gorgeous, spectacular, awesome, stunning, dazzling, and majestic could not begin to describe this area. The region's resplendent landscape with its endless rolling lush green hills and fields dotted with tea leaves/plants and waterfalls were a real treat for the eyes. It was forever memorable!!

The blue train chugged on passing plantations in the misty fog. I heard screams as the train went through a tunnel. I heard them again when we went through another tunnel. It turned out that they were made by young boys on the train. Were they OK? I went to investigate. A group of boys laughed when they saw me. They were A-OK. I then realized that screaming was the thing to do on trains in Sri Lanka. We all screamed at the top of our lungs when the train went through the next tunnel. I felt like a kid again! It felt great to immerse myself in the local culture. Welcome to life in Sri Lanka!

Nomadic food merchants selling Sri Lankan snacks came on board at station stops along the way. Sweet and savory food such as small buns stuffed with exotic fillings and whole mangoes were offered to me. Nuts were sprinkled with colorful spices and served in newspaper cones. Vendors quickly conducted their trading and hopped off seconds before the halfway hanging off the platform railway guard waved his green flag. Seconds later, the train slowly pulled away chugging forward into the hills hillier than the ones present in Saint Lucia, a Windward Island in the Caribbean Sea.

Most of the "slower than slow" journey was spent just watching life going on around me punctuated by gorgeous scenery. The only bump in the road was caused by bumps in the road. While I loved Sri Lankan curries, I hated them, too! Or the upset stomach I had from eating one before embarking on this long and bumpy train ride. It was like feeling motion sick or seasick. The devil was in the details and I had not thought of every detail in planning this excursion.

However, as a prepared traveler, my always present diarrhea pills, a bottle of water, and some crackers I had in my bag, provided some much needed relief. Hours later, I regained my strength, endurance, and chugged on along with the little blue train with our "know we can" positive attitude.

Once we arrived in the general area, I took a bus and then another bus for about 20 minutes total for 46 LKR to Pedro Tea Factory. It cost 200 LKR for a 20-minute tour of the factory. Our tour guide gave us green smocks to wear over our clothes as the factory was quite dusty. No photographs could be taken in the factory except for a bin of tea leaves. He showed us the drying, rolling, cutting, cleaning, and grading rooms. Both men and women worked in the factory. We saw clean tea and unclean tea. After the tour, we were served a cup of Ceylon tea accompanied by a cracker in a dining room with scenic views.

When tea-time was over, I headed to the tea fields where I met some very hard-working female tea pluckers who did back-breaking work! They wore long deep cone shaped baskets on their backs which caught the newly plucked tea leaves that they threw over their shoulders. Wearing baskets in front would have posed major logistical problems.

After seeing how hard they work so that we can enjoy a daily cuppa, I will never take one for granted. I repeatedly thanked the girls for all their efforts in an exuberant and appreciative tone. I'm not sure if they knew what I was saying, but they smiled at me. I just needed to let them know that without them many people would not be able to keep calm and carry on.

I left tea country on a bus to Kandy which took about 2-3/4 hours, quickly ate some KFC, and got a seat in a commuter van headed to Colombo. I wanted to give my stomach a rest from anymore bumps but was not prepared for the million stops we made for 3-1/2 hours. Getting glimpses of local commuter life in the letting-offs and picking-ups of office workers en route to Colombo was most enlightening. I spoke with a teacher and an accountant and enjoyed learning about life here. Mixing up modes of transportation is vital when on the road to get a "real feel" for a place. I encountered waterfalls, hills dotted with tea plants, drop dead gorgeous scenery, female tea pickers, and local commuters. It was a great day trip even with a few bumps along the way. Worth it!!!!

(May 2017)

Tea Country Tip: Visit the Lover's Leap waterfall.

ASIA

JAPAN

Faking it with Plastic Food

Food foreplay is a way of life in Japan. Plastic food displays grace the front windows of most Japanese restaurants. Buyer Beware: WYSIWYG. The positive thing about "foodie show & tell" is that you can complain if anything is left out of your order. The proof is in the pudding, I mean the plastic!

It's all there from chirashi, edamame, miso soup, omurice, onigiri, ramen, rice, sashimi, soba, many types of sushi (inari, gunkan, maki, nigiri, oshizushi, sasazushi, temaki, and temari), tempura, tonkatsu, udon, yakitori, gari, wasabi, and mochi for dessert.

Even the "eyes bigger than your stomach" 6-15 multi-course kaiseki dinner and bento boxes with their detailed, precise, and aesthetic presentation are there to tempt your taste buds. It's all a real treat for the four senses (taste, see, smell, and touch) and all five senses (hear) if you order a sizzling hot dish.

Itadakimasu!

Osaka
CUPNOODLES MUSEUM

After years of eating instant cup noodles for economic or convenience reasons, a stop at the noodle museum in Osaka **(cupnoodles-museum.jp)** AKA Momofuku Ando Instant Ramen Museum was a must.

I learned oodles about noodles and product packaging & design as I strolled through the instant noodles tunnel. It reminded me a bit of the Museum of Brands in London but with a noodle focus. Be sure to go inside the tiny rustic work shed to see where it all began. Momofuku's dedication to making his invention become a reality has impacted so many lives.

You only fork over some yen if you want to design a soup cup or immerse yourself in making chicken ramen in an orange & white industrial and futuristic looking Jetsons like kitchen. You'll knead, spread, steam, and dry ramen, etc.

The free museum in Osaka Ikeda is about a 45-minute drive from Kyoto or a brief walk from the Hankyu Takarazuka Line Ikeda Station. *(December 2018)*

Thanks, Momofuku, for oodles of noodles!

Tip: The museum might be closed on Tuesdays.

Years ago, on a flight from the UK to Australia, I observed a rather lopsided and bulging pallet filled with noodle packs going through customs. What kind of traveler ships stuff like that? And why? Will wonders never cease? Noodles are cheap and easily found anywhere and everywhere unlike Marmite® which is like gold dust in some parts of the world. What was the savings benefit if you had to pay hefty customs duties or excess baggage fees to transport all those oodles of noodles? Go figure!

It all made sense years later when I watched a customs program on TV in the UK. A border agent/customs officer noticed some messy glue work on a few of many noodle packs. They were either glued together by a newbie to the glue gun process or glued towards the end of a shift by a weary worker. Unfortunately, those messy seams aroused suspicion. The suspect ones were opened, scanned, and found to have more than just noodles in there. Agatha Christie would have been impressed. I sure hope that that customs officer got a good promotion.

Tokyo
Ordering Noodles via a Vending Machine

A few hours after I arrived in Tokyo, checked into the Oak Hostel Zen, took a hot shower, and a jet lag recovery nap if there is such a thing; I went in search of noodles.

It's not easy to suppress hunger pains in Japan where most restaurants display "plastic Japanese fake food" in their front windows. At this point, I was "Hank Marvin" which means starving in Cockney rhyming slang. I felt like I could go into the opposite state of a food coma at any minute but needed to hunt around a bit more to avoid any food FOMO. After walking on the main street for a few minutes, I ventured off the beaten path and turned down a side street. That street led to an alley and that alley led to a crooked lane with some interesting looking shops and restaurants. Touristy areas in Tokyo tend to have street signs in Japanese & English but some residential neighborhoods have them in Japanese only. Unfortunately, I know nothing about Japanese scripts, symbols, and characters. Fortunately, I know quite a bit about Japanese food!

And then I saw it! At the end of the lane was a tiny wooden and rustic looking restaurant that looked like it had been there since before the Edo period. Its curtain was down but its front door was open so hungry and crazy old me made a beeline for it as fast as I could.

Once inside, I spotted a hip young Japanese male cook who quickly and discretely made eye contact with me. He did not speak English and I did not speak any Japanese, so it was a bit of a "lost in translation" moment when I tried to order. I resorted to making a charade like gesture in which I brought the invisible spoon that I held in my right hand up to my open mouth a few times. I think he finally got the message as he pointed to a nearby ticket vending machine which I went over to. Its buttons featured Japanese characters. Once again, it was another "lost in translation" moment where the resulting ordered menu item would be a complete and utter surprise.

Since it was lunchtime, I didn't have to wait too long before another diner entered. I watched as he put some yen into the vending machine, pushed a button, and received a ticket from it which he gave to the cook. I confidently did the exact same thing he did and handed my ticket with Japanese characters on it to the cook, too. What did I just order??

The cook got busy stirring broth in a huge old cooking pot which he added noodles to. He stirred and stirred. About ten minutes later, he served the customer who had ordered before me. He looked very content as he hungrily sipped away at his soup which put my mind at ease. About two minutes later, the cook served me a bowl of the same soup, chock full of chubby udon noodles in a clear broth with veggies and a few types of mushrooms.

Some noodle soup connoisseurs think that the secret of noodle soup is in the broth while others say it is in the noodles. I think that the magic is the marriage of both ingredients. A Double Happiness! I happily sipped my tasty mystery soup with its secret broth and slippery silky noodles. Never slurp soup.

I have no idea what I sipped or where I sipped it at, but I think I could find the little restaurant again. It would be nice to come to Tokyo again, hopefully, during cherry blossom season. Although, the red, orange, and yellow autumn leaves were breathtakingly beautiful.

(November 2015)

Tokyo Ramen Tip: Go to Tsuta for Michelin-starred ramen noodles.

Good Luck Trip Japan (Tokyo & Other Cities) gltjp.com

Tokyo

Jiro Dreams of Sushi

After watching the documentary "Jiro Dreams of Sushi," it went on the bucket list for Things to Do in Tokyo.

Jiro is impossibly hard to get a reservation at and eating there is not cheap. However, it is supposed to be an incredible sushi experience. Eat every grain of rice to get your money's worth! The omakase tasting menu (the chef decides on the dishes to make) costs 40,000 yen or about $375 plus tax. (Price quote as of 2020). Tipping is not really done in Japan so at least you'll save some yen.

After a full day of sightseeing in Tokyo including a very early morning stop at the famous Tsukiji fish market, I made my way to Sukiyabashi Jiro (sushi-jiro.jp). It's located near the Ginza subway station in a basement of all places. Strange, right? Right! That is exactly what I thought! At least they can attract the well to do commuter crowd. After wandering around for about ten minutes, I was lost and needed help. Jiro was hidden. It was time to seek out a blingy passerby who looked like they could afford to eat there and ask for directions. After a few unsuccessful encounters, a businessman who looked like he was in the know did know! He gave me directions and after sensing my uneasiness in finding it even with them, he escorted me there.

Once I was briefly inside this sacred sushi spot, I spotted Jiro Ono at the sushi counter talking to a few male customers. There were less than a dozen counter seats and a few tables. They all subtly noticed me after Jiro discretely looked at me first. I asked the hostess if I could eat dinner then. She asked if I had a reservation, and I said no which led her to saying "NO" in a kind but firm tone. One can always try!

I was still able to experience a little bit of Jiro sushi in the form of a small paperback book that I bought for a few yen. On the way back to my capsule hotel, I thought about Jiro's sushi that I saw from afar. Perhaps one of the secret ingredients in serving stellar sushi is having a sushi joint not far from a fresh fish market? The trip had been well worth it to get a sneak peek at Jiro's operation.

Do not wear strong perfume here. That is a big No. It is probably safer not to wear any.

Tokyo Sushi Tip: Jiro's son owns a restaurant in Roppongi Hills. Closed on Wednesdays?

Tokyo

Sushi for Breakfast?

"Sushi for breakfast?"

Over the years, I have been a crazy mixed-up tourist just going with the "cultural foodie flow" eating omelettes and crêpes for dinner in Paris and now sushi for breakfast in Tokyo.

One morning around 10 AM, I went to the Tsukiji wholesale fish market where I toured the outer market but missed the 6 AM tuna auction. Only 120 lucky tourists that line up a few hours before its start get to see all the live action.

I like certain food for breakfast and sushi is not one of them. That's for lunch and dinner in my world. But then I remembered that I had traveled halfway around the world to see the world, so found myself eating a variety of very fresh sushi for breakfast! I don't think I could have eaten it at 6 AM and 2 PM would have been ideal but no way was I going to have sushi FOMO in Japan. No way!! *(November 2015)*

Tokyo Market Tip: Visit the new Toyosu Market **(shijou.metro.tokyo.lg.jp)** as this has replaced Tsukiji market with the tuna auction at 5:30 AM.

HONG KONG

A Tea Lover's Paradise

I ducked out of the monsoon like rains one afternoon in Kowloon as I had done many other times that week, but this time, I found myself thrust into a tea lover's paradise. The sign said a tea salon and shop, Tea WG, at Elements. And what a wonderful tea shop it was! I felt like a kid in a candy store!

The walls were lined with many large yellow metal containers labeled with fabulous flavors such as Happy Birthday Tea, Literary Tea, My Favourite Tea, Paris Breakfast Tea, Rose Boudoir Tea, and Sweet France Tea. How great are these names? Check out their other teas at **twgtea.com and teawg.com**.

I finally understood what the expression, "Not for all the tea in China," meant as there was no way I was leaving Hong Kong without a bag of Lucky loose-leaf tea at the very least.

London Tea Buying Tip: TWG Tea, Harrod's in Knightsbridge, and Fortnum & Mason near Piccadilly Circus/Green Park sell all kinds of lovely teas.

(January 2016)

THAILAND

Bangkok

Insects Anyone?

It was almost midnight as I was exiting my cab with my suitcase, an always awkward process, when I was immediately accosted by scorpions. Scorpions?? Yes. Scorpions!!

A young male Thai street vendor thrust about a dozen skewers of some very scary looking grilled insects right before my very own eyes. They were coated in an orangey red BBQ sauce and were lined up like soldiers in a square white plastic tray. Between this and Bangkok's sweltering heat, it was all a bit too much and too up close and personal for me. I did not feel like smiling in the Land of Smiles right now.

I waved my hand a few times as an urgent sign and request for him to step back with whatever frightening things he was trying to sell me. He got the hint and distanced himself from me as I caught my breath, calmed down, and asked him what they were. "Scorpions," he said. Just as I thought. I told him, "Thanks, but no thanks!" I quickly made my way towards my accommodation trying to avoid similar contact with street food vendors, Thai massage promoters, and many drunk & rowdy backpackers along the way. It reminded me a bit of the Venice Beach Boardwalk in Southern CA.

I had heard about the craziness of Khao San Road, however, I had to see it for myself. Seeing really is believing!!!! Although it was a chaotic street, it was less than 2 km from the Grand Palace and some other wats (temples) so an ideal location.

On the way to the hostel, I passed another vendor selling similar creatures who said they were eels when I inquired. To tell you the truth, my stomach could not handle and did not want to eat either. I thanked him, walked away without buying any and Googled scorpions on my smartphone. They sure looked like the ones I didn't buy. I was born in November and my zodiac sign is Scorpio. That means I had just rejected one of my own. I could only hope my future horoscopes would not forecast hunger, scorpions, or rejection. Although, writers experience rejection and I have managed to handle that with a tenacious attitude.

Anyway, I watched him walk up and down the short and crowded strip approaching and surprising other tourists in a similar manner. I didn't see anyone buy anything, but the night was still young. I, on the other hand, was not so young, so called it a night with my stomach intact.

About 2 weeks before leaving London for Asia; I had visited the Natural History Museum in South Kensington. The Creepy Crawlies gallery there had a weird but neat insect (arthropods) vending machine.

Insect eating is a way of life in some Asian countries as they're rich in protein. The Japanese eat grasshoppers and insect eating was popular in the Edo period. I think I could eat a grasshopper if it were a life-or-death situation or if I were out of my mind. Desperate times call for desperate measures! I know I do not have the stomach or the nerve to eat a wiggly and furry caterpillar. Not for me, no thanks! My mother told me that in 1940 when she was a kid in NJ, that some kids ate chocolate covered ants.

On past travels, I have picked an insect or two out of bowls of rice or noodles but just sucked it up and dived in as I was starving and was unsure when I would eat again. I have found hairs in my food in the USA which made me wonder if it is easier to eat an insect or a hair. I really do not want to eat either.

I made it out of there alive the next morning and saw some lovely wats. Wat, I mean what, could be better than seeing one Buddhist temple after another?

(May 2017)

Bangkok

Food at the Floating Markets

Thailand is known for its floating markets and food stalls. Long boats loaded with exotic and ordinary fruits & veggies for sale glide down the river making for a most epicurean sight! Damnoen Saduak, in Ratchaburi Province, about 60 miles from Bangkok is a very famous market.

Since this culture vulture had some time constraints, I jumped on a rickety yet functional Bangkok bus and arrived at Taling Chan one hour later. It's a smaller market than the other ones and most of the wooden boats are docked instead of free floating. The front stalls sold flowers, produce, noodles, desserts, snacks, and textiles while the boats docked in the back sold hot & cold traditional Thai dishes and salads.

During my self-guided foodie tour, fiery red, bright emerald green, sunny yellow and orangey orange chili peppers were spotted. There were even purple chili peppers which surprised the heck out of me. Imagine that! Purple chili peppers!! I wondered what their spiciness/heat measurement was on the Scoville Heat Scale. Were they hotter than the Carolina Reaper?

Local food vendors busied themselves setting up their makeshift kitchens and firing up their grills and stoves. They chopped all sorts of fresh veggies that they blended into orange-colored soups and yellow curries housed in large cooking pots. I watched a Thai lady whose very delicate facial features were protected from the sun by a Thai farmer's hat (ngob) as she grilled silvery whole fishes on wooden skewers. She patiently turned crabs and prawns/shrimp over smoking and glowing red-orange coals. She served them on a plate along with a few sauces on the side and a veggie salad to hungry waiting customers.

Thailand Market Tips: Taling Chan was only open on Saturdays and Sundays when I went in May 2017. Bring Thai Baht.

Bang Nam Phueng Floating Market, a small riverside food market, near Bangkok is popular with the locals. Open on Saturday & Sunday only?

Khlong Lat Mayom is a floating market just a few miles outside Bangkok. Open on Saturday & Sunday only?

Hom Hostel & Cooking Club

I found myself lost in both a location way and a lost in translation way when I tried to make sense of directions to Hom Hostel & Cooking Club. I arrived at a small shopping center in Bangkok thinking surely, it can't be in here? Why would a hostel be in a shopping center? It just seemed a bit odd and more than likely a big misunderstanding on my part. Although, travel has taught me that the journey can be just as important and interesting as the destination. I nomadically wandered around some more and eventually located it on the fourth floor. And was I ever glad that I stayed the course, as an amazing foodie experience was in store for me! The friendly staff, scenic roof top, herb garden, and clean hostel made for a memorable experience for about 13 GBP or $17.00! *(May 2017)*

Hom **(homcookinghostel.com)** is a must stop for any aspiring chef or foodie wanting to learn Thai cooking! Hom offers private rooms, dorm room beds, and a free cooking demo for hostel guests. In addition, cooking classes are available for a fee where students receive hands on instruction on how to prepare two Thai dishes from their very own cookbook. Other types of classes are offered, too.

Thai Food & Drink in Plastic Bags

Hot, humid, steamy, and sticky Bangkok is chock-full of street food stalls, day & night markets, and a few floating markets. For a few THB (Thai Baht) you will be spoiled for choice with Thai prawn crackers, green papaya salad, chicken satay, Tom yum soup, Thai curry noodles, Pad Thai, green curry, red curry, Pad Krapow Gai (Spicy Thai basil chicken), and fried rice, etc.

OMG!! OMG!! What's in those plastic bags? Salads, fresh-cut fruit, juices, and sodas are packaged in clear plastic bags and sold on the streets of Bangkok!! And to think for all these years, I thought that only goldfish could be transported in see through plastic bags!

Handy Dandy Tip: Do not wear white clothes or your best/favorite outfit when carrying Thai street food anywhere in Thailand.

Bangkok Tip: Train Night Market Ratchada **(facebook.com/taradrodfi.ratchada)** is open every day from 5 PM – 1 AM. A good selection of Thai & Western street food is available. Handcrafted and hip like goods are sold, too.

SINGAPORE

Chewing Gum was Banned?

In 1992, Singapore banned chewing gum as the country, city, and island nation wanted nice & neat public spaces and fully functional mass transit. Since I am not a gum addict, resident, or a frequent visitor other than making a pit stop at Changi Airport on the way to Australia every few years, the gum ban didn't affect me too much. Although, it would be nice if my local dreary and boring airports in the UK and USA could be more like Changi, which is exceptional. It really is! Why don't more airports have a butterfly garden, cactus garden, orchid garden, sunflower garden, and movie theater? It's no wonder it has won awards for being the World's Best Airport.

So best to check current laws if you're a gum chewer and plan on visiting or transiting through The Lion City. There might be exceptions for medicinal or dental gum. I'm sure Astrid or Eleanor from the movie/book "Crazy Rich Asians" could get away with gum smuggling or anything for that matter. It would be tough to live with a Chardonnay ban, but at least with a gum ban, I won't get any sticky soles. Yeah!!

Crazy Rich Asians: Where Does Astrid Eat?

After reading the book and seeing the movie, "Crazy Rich Asians," I became a bit obsessed with where "It Girl" Astrid might eat in Asia. On trips to Singapore and Hong Kong, I looked for chic and child friendly foodie spots that would be worthy of her patronage.

Singapore: Do you think she meets girlfriends for a Singapore Sling at Raffles? Does she eat rice at one of the many hawker centres or bowls of Katong laksa (noodle soup) at 328 Katong Laksa? Do you think Michael or HNW Charlie and her eat at Waku Ghin at Marina Bay Sands? They probably don't need reservations since her powerful grandmother, Ah Ma, owns almost everything on the island nation. She must take her son to Lickety for ice cream and waffles. Do they buy ice cream from an ice cream truck like normal people do if they're over on Sentosa island trying to cool off from Singapore's tropical climate?

Hong Kong: Does she eat dinner with Charlie at Amber or Caprice? Does she take her son on the Star Ferry with locals and tourists so that he can have a normal childhood? Or does she charter a private junk boat to ferry them across Victoria Harbour?

AUSTRALIA

The Avocado Farmer in Queensland

Avocados for sale. That's what the farmer's hand-made sign that we had just passed advertised. "Stop! Stop! Please Stop!!" My screaming stop at the top of my lungs put my "no worries" Aussie mates into a state of shock.

We had just pulled out of the rustic Boomerang Farm (boomerangfarm.com.au) in Mudgeeraba where they tried to play 9 holes of golf. Unfortunately, a few kangaroos had other plans for their golf balls as they hopped onto the course, scooped them up, put them into their pockets, and victoriously hopped away. They would make ideal Deliveroo drivers someday.

After making their golf fantasies a reality, it was time to satisfy my food fantasy with a pit stop right then right there. Thoughts of all the ways I could use that green superfood flashed through my mind. Visions of guacamole and chips accompanied by a margarita seemed like an ideal and always welcome option. Years later, smashed avocado on toast would be a viable competitor. I only wished I had the patience of a sushi chef to whip up California rolls or avocado & cucumber rolls in a zen-like state.

I jumped out of the car before it came to a full stop and ran back to where the farmer was standing.

I peeked into one of the many brown paper bags that were sprawled out on the table. There were more than 20 ripe avocados in it! I went into price shock when he told me a bag cost 5 AUD.

Only 5 AUD? OMG!! The AUD currency exchange rate against the USD in September 2001 meant that they cost next to nothing. He was basically giving them away at that price. Most of the time, my avocado buying was a case of highway robbery and very disappointing, also. Grocery store avocados were either pricey, unripe, or both. Although, I did get lucky at times at the farmer's market in NYC's Union Square.

I gladly and excitedly paid the avocado farmer a bit more than 5 AUD for the bag, as that was all I had on me and he didn't have any change. This deal was a steal! Feeling like both a big spender and a true Aussie, I told him to keep the change. "No worries, mate," I said as I ran back to the car hugging my paper bag chock-full of loot. I mean fruit. And then it was back to the Gold Coast with my newly acquired jackpot. There'd be no need to hit a pokie (slot machine) club on the way home as I had already had a big fruit win!

The Works Burger & The Freakshake

I was warned but went ahead anyway. My mates told me to share one. They were not kidding! "The Works Burger" made a Big Mac® and Whopper® seem teeny tiny. I bet them I could finish one. I lost the bet!

In September 2001, some mates took me to the Tweed Valley to see the Natural Bridge. It's a popular outdoorsy attraction on the Gold Coast with its scenic waterfall and small cave with glow-worms. There are bats there, too. The plan was to hike first to build up an appetite and then have lunch at the Valley View Café. Mission accomplished! Two hours later, we had seen some beautiful natural scenery, glowing glow-worms, and bats hanging upside down fast asleep from afar. Time to eat!!

"The Works Burger" was huge, enormous, gigantic, humongous, and mega big. This supersized super-duper burger consisted of lettuce, tomato, ketchup, mustard, a fried egg, a pineapple ring, beetroot, onion, cheese, bacon, and a hamburger patty. There might have been some avocado in it, too. I was surprised there was not a glow-worm in it. A vegetarian could it eat it without the bacon and hamburger patty, etc.

After not finishing it all, "as my eyes were bigger than my stomach," I finally understood how the burger got its name. A lot of work went into making it. A lot of work went into eating it. Eight years later I returned there but shared one since I knew better.

Those Aussies are really something with their biggie culinary creations! The Freakshake, a huge messy milkshake, originated Down Under in Canberra, but quickly spread to other countries.

While a milkshake has billions of calories, the monstrous Freakshake has gazillions of calories as it's packed with all types of sweets and brownie chunks. I tried one at Molly Bakes (permanently closed now) in London's Dalston area a few years ago which put me in a sugar shock for the rest of the day. I bet an Aussie would say, "No worries, mate, just calories!"

There's no way anyone could eat a Works Burger and a Freakshake in the same sitting or even on the same day. No way!! I don't even think that Morgan Spurlock from the documentary, "Super Size Me," could eat them both on the same day without going into a calorific food coma.

CARIBBEAN

Jamaica
Chicken Gumbo or Chikungunya?

After weeks of dreaming about reggae, rum, and jerk chicken, the plane finally touched down in Kingston.

The afternoon was full of everything you would hope for and expect for a "fun in the sun" destination. Of course, negative factors such as clouds, rain, time spent awkwardly applying suntan lotion, and trying to find a comfy lounge chair position are to be expected.

Life really can't get any better when you're busy chillaxing and relaxing to island songs such as "Escape," AKA "The Pina Colada Song" and every song by Bob Marley or The Beach Boys.

After a few hours of sunbathing and watching the sun set in shades of skybluepink, I realized I was starving. The cold and creamy piña colada I had enjoyed earlier didn't satisfy the hunger I felt now. I quickly changed into all white clothing, tried to calm down my hair that had gotten a bit frizzy from the island heat, and proceeded up to the hotel's rooftop restaurant. I already knew what I wanted to eat but read the menu anyway to avoid any menu FOMO. I could have ackee and saltfish, Jamaican beef patties, plantains, callaloo, coco bread, rice & peas, roti, or curry goat. I ordered jerk chicken, spicy rice, and a piña colada.

Next to my table sat a lively family of five from Kingston and Miami who chatted, laughed, and joked with each other before their conversation turned more serious after a while. I could not help but hear them since they spoke so loudly and were so close by. They kept talking about the chicken gumbo and how it was bad if you got it. I didn't remember seeing any gumbo on the menu which made my mind run wild. Did the gumbo get discontinued because it gave people food poisoning? That would make sense. Surely, that is what they must mean.

My jerk chicken finally arrived and didn't disappoint with its "jerky" flavor. The environment/atmosphere where food is served/eaten plays such a big part in the gastronomic experience. Palm trees and steel drum music add as much flavor as a jerk seasoning made from cayenne pepper, garlic, onions, brown sugar, thyme, and allspice, etc. However, I wouldn't turn down any jerk on a cold and dreary winter night in London (Brixton).

Although I was thoroughly enjoying my jerk, all their getting sick from gumbo talk was starting to "Jamaican me crazy." Thankfully, my prayers were answered when they started talking about who was making what for tomorrow's breakfast. They argued over whose ackee & saltfish recipe was better. The first time I ate ackee was 20 years ago on a trip to Negril. It's a fruit whose cooked flesh looks like scrambled eggs. This went on for a few minutes until a couple stopped by their table and asked how Laticia was feeling. Again, chicken gumbo was mentioned.

About a minute later, the nightly news came on with reports of more cases of chicken gumbo. Treatment advice and a health hotline number flashed on the TV screen. It turned out that chicken gumbo was Chikungunya, a virus from mosquito bites which causes a fever, bad headaches, and arthritic joints.

Fortunately, I had sprayed a double dose of citronella mosquito repellent all over my body. I only hoped I had covered all its nooks and crannies, if that's at all possible, before I went to dine al fresco. Past trips to the Caribbean and India taught me to wear white or pastel colored clothing, as dark colors attract mosquitoes. Leave your black bikini home! Try not to sweat either. Just another day in paradise! Paradise!! Paradise!! *(October 2014)*

USA Health Tip: (CDC) (cdc.gov)
UK Health Tip: fitfortravel.nhs.uk

Saint Lucia
Bananas & Banana Ketchup

On a very scenic and hilly ride from Hewanorra International Airport to my hotel, I noticed many blue plastic bags in the trees. Sensing that I might ask him about them, the taxi driver beat me to it. He explained that bananas were a big export business for Saint Lucia and were used to make banana ketchup, too. The bags were used to delay ripening and to protect the bananas from insects and from getting their exterior (banana skin/peel) bruised. I'm not one for excessive plastic bag use, but who wants a bruised banana?

Banana ketchup? Hmm!! It's a case of when life gives you bananas, you make banana ketchup. Simple! The tomato-less ketchup is concocted from banana pulp, garlic, onion, salt, vinegar, water, and spices. You really learn something new every day! My foodie curious and curiouser tried a few versions of it at various island restaurants. Some were mellow while others were sweet.

You can pick up some homemade banana hot sauce in a variety of flavors (tangy, spicy, or hot) at the market in Castries.

Island Food & Drink
Cacao Beans and Chocolate

Cacao beans and chocolate in the hot Caribbean sun? Wouldn't they melt? It's very hard to believe that cacao beans/pods from trees flourish in hot tropical climates such as Dominican Republic, Jamaica, Saint Lucia and Martinique in the Caribbean, Mexico, Brazil, Ecuador, and Peru in South America, Sri Lanka, and Malaysia. Who would have thought? Go figure!!

Saint Lucia Chocolate Hotel/Restaurant Tip:
Boucan by Hotel Chocolat in Soufriere

From a Coconut to Coconut Water

It didn't matter which Caribbean island I bought a coconut on, as they all seemed to be sold from the back of a beat up old pickup truck or a rickety wheelbarrow. The coconut vendors were always local guys with long braided hair or hair that bulged out from underneath a knit cap in the Rasta colors of black, green, gold, and red.

In 2014-2016, they cost either 2 XCD $ in Saint Lucia or St. Vincent, 150 Jamaican $ in Jamaica, 2 Bajan $ in Barbados, so about 90 pence or $1.25. Quick hydration with au naturel coconut water right from the source is much cheaper here than in the UK and USA where it costs a pretty penny and comes in a bottle or a box.

Besides getting coconut juice for a bargain, I got free entertainment, too. The vendor would casually whack off the top of the coconut with his sharp knife. Customers were always asked if they wanted a straw or if they wanted to drink the coconut water from a bag? I always drank it straight from the coconut to be more green and eco-conscious. Once finished, I would hand the coconut back to the coconut vendor. He would effortlessly chop it in half and make a crude but useable spoon from the coconut shell. He would give you the spoon and the coconut so that you could scoop out the jelly (pulp) for an extra treat.

On a sunny day in Saint Lucia after drinking some coconut water and right before eating some coconut pulp; the vendor told me it was good for the wood. I had no idea what he was talking about until he pointed to his covered private part between his legs. I think he meant something a bit fresh. I quickly thanked him and went on my way far away from him, his knife, and ready, waiting & willing wood.

This too up close and personal incident really made me appreciate the professionalism of a coconut water vendor at Going Nuts outside the Norman Manley International Airport in Kingston, Jamaica in late 2014. I ordered, paid for, and received my coconut water in its shell. I was grateful for the absence of any coconutty remarks and the pointing to any private part! He smiled at me, I smiled back at him, and was off to catch my flight.

Every Island has Their Own Beer

There's a local beer wherever you go in the Caribbean to quench your thirst as you relax and watch the sun set.

Bahamas-Kalik
Barbados and Guyana-Banks
Dominican Republic-Presidente
Dominica-Kubuli
Guadeloupe-Gwada Gold
Jamaica-Red Stripe
Martinique-Biere Lorraine
St. Lucia-Piton
Grenada, St. Kitts, Trinidad & Tobago-Carib
St. Vincent & the Grenadines-Hairoun

Every Island has Their Own Rum

Many islands make rum because they grow sugarcane. They tend to have distillery tours for revenue generating and entertainment purposes.

Antigua & Barbuda-English Harbour
Barbados-Mount Gay
St. Lucia-Chairman's Reserve
USVI-St. Croix-Cruzan & St. Thomas-Bones.
Cheers!!

EUROPE

AUSTRIA

Vienna

Sachertorte & Viennese Coffeehouses

Indulging in a slice of chocolate cake and a cup of coffee at a Viennese café or coffeehouse is a must do when in the cake & coffee city of Wien (Vienna). Taking a bite of this decadent cake is like eating a piece of Austrian history, as it caused a bit of a stir here years ago regarding its creator. The Original Sacher-Torte can be enjoyed at Café Sacher and a version of it, Demel's Sachertorte, at Demel.

"Let them eat Sachertorte!" And that is exactly what I planned to do, but even the best laid plans can go awry. Any cake dreams crumbled after I saw the long line outside the café. If I stood in it, I would miss out on seeing all that Vienna had to offer such as Schönbrunn Palace, Architekturzentrum Wien, MuseumsQuartier (MQ), and Micromuseums & Passages in the Q21/MQ, etc.

Who needs any gooey chocolatey desserts? I DO!! My wish came true a few seconds later when I spotted a nearby kiosk that sold slices and whole cakes eliminating any foodie FOMO. I was overjoyed with the joy of missing out (JOMO) on having to stand in a long line.

I popped into the kiosk and five minutes later, I left with a small Bordeaux red colored shopping bag imprinted with gold letters and gold rope handles. It looked like I had bought some very expensive jewelry and not just a cake cube for 4.90 Euros.

I hated to unbox the Original Sacher Cube, but out it came right into my ready and waiting mouth where it was quickly but consciously devoured. There was no way I could take a cake side. I was time poor and could not possibly taste the other one that day without going into a chocolate coma. And then I was off, as there was no way this culture vulture was going to miss visiting mumok and the Leopold Museum.

(November 2017)

Perhaps leave the coffee cup with the iconic green design for when you're back home and enjoy your Brauner (espresso), Melange (cappuccino), or Einspänner somewhere like Alt Wien Kaffee, Café Central, Café Drechsler, or Kleines Café? Or at Café Sperlhof which has tons of board games.

Check out Coffeehouse Conversations (spaceandplace.at) for events which pair up a local & a tourist.

Vienna Information Tip: wien.info

BULGARIA

That's a Bottle of Beer?

What the heck is that? Soda? No. Beer? Yes, beer! That's a bottle of beer. Beer!!

I couldn't believe my eyes when I spotted several bulging 1.5 L and 2.5 L plastic bottles filled with amber and golden colored liquids (beer) in many stores and kleks (kneel down shops) in Sofia and Bansko. They were cheap as chips, too! Prices ranged from around 1.50 BGN or 2.50 BGN (about 75 pence to 1.50 GBP or $1 to $1.50). Trust me, I wasn't under the influence and imaging these prices! The whole country was affordable!

I felt "happy-sad" on the flight back to the UK. It is one of the few times that I Lev, I mean left, somewhere with change in my pocket and felt like a big spender. Although I wasn't crazy about the stray dogs there, I love roses and Bulgaria is known for its roses!

(September 2017)

CROATIA

The Zero-Waste Orange

Waiting tables in my younger days to make money for a backpacking trip to Europe, I saw a lot of waste, unfortunately. Years later, trips to India showed me what real starvation looks like.

On a winter's day in Dubrovnik, in a country that grows oranges like Spain & like the states of Florida and California, I really understood the concept of food and zero-waste. Not only do the sweet bitter orangey oranges grown here decorate this wild and naturally beautiful place, they can be eaten in two ways, also.

Two ways to eat an orange? Yes. First you peel it and enjoy its orangey flesh segments (endocarp and carpel). Then you make candied orange peel strips (arancini). Ta-da!! The zero-waste orange! Those Croatians sure know how to get their Kunas worth!

(December 2018)

visitdubrovnik.hr

CZECH REPUBLIC

Karlovy Vary
Becherovka's Secret Recipe

A desire to get a better view of the curvy shaped spa town, Karlovy Vary, had me climbing up a mountain one afternoon. I would either struggle up it or slide down it. About 30 minutes later, I felt frustrated and afraid. Why had I put my arms and legs in jeopardy like this especially since I avoid skiing to protect them?

I gingerly soldiered on and made it to the top unscathed. I spotted a restaurant, Jeleni Skok, so ran inside as I really had to use the bathroom. I hadn't planned on drinking so early in the day, but my nerves were officially shot and if I ate or drank something then I could use the toilet for free. Many places in this country charge 10 CZK to use the toilet. I ordered a shot of Becherovka to save some Korunas. This 200+ year old secret recipe herbal liqueur with a spicy and cinnamon flavor can be enjoyed as a shot or in a cocktail like a Beton. Some people think that drinking it is good for their digestive system. It calmed my nerves! A tour at the Jan Becher Museum includes a tasting of a few drinks from the brand. **(becherovka.cz).** *(November 2017)*

ESTONIA

Marzipan & Onions

KALEV MARZIPAN ROOM IN TALLINN

Who would have thought that marzipan was a medicine of sorts many years ago? A trip to this tiny museum at Pikk 16 in Tallinn's Old Town confirmed that there's so much more to this almondy sweet than eating it coated in chocolate or in the shape of a colorful fruit or veggie!

Tallinn Tip: tallinn.inyourpocket.com

ESTONIA'S ONION ROUTE

An onion route? You've got to see it to believe it!

You'll be an Old Believer after you see miles and miles of these very historic golden onions!

Estonia Tip: visitestonia.com

FRANCE

French Sweets that Start with C & M

Many French sweets begin with the letters C and M such as Canelés, Clafoutis, Crêpes, Crème Brûlée, Crème Caramel, Macarons, Madeleines, Meringues, and Mousse. And then there are Éclairs, Galettes, Gateaux, Palmiers, Soufflès, and Tartes!

Paris
Macarons not Macaroons

Macaroons are coconut cookies while Macarons are double layered meringue and almond based round sweet treats. Always spell and pronounce Macaron correctly as if you spell or say it as Macron people will think you're referring to Emmanuel who's been France's President since 2017.

Macarons are mostly petite in size and usually come in pastel colors. Typical flavors are caramel, chocolate, coffee, lavender, lemon, mint, orange, pistachio, raspberry, rose, strawberry, vanilla & violet.

Macaron Shopping in Paris:
Many Parisian patisseries, Monoprix & international chains such as Ladurée Paris, Pierre Hermé & PAUL sell them.

Macaron Shopping Elsewhere:

EUROPE

GREECE
Naxos
AKTAION pastry boutique
aktaio.com
Pretty macarons.

ITALY
Verona
Flego Pasticceria *(A few locations in Verona.)*

USA
MI
Detroit (Corktown)
Lucky Detroit Finely Crafted Coffee & Espresso
luckydetroit.com

Paris

Chocolat Chaud at Angelina

Imagine drinking a very rich chocolate bar.

Well, thanks to Angelina (**angelina-paris.fr**) at 226 Rue de Rivoli near Place Vendôme in the 1st arrondissement, you can. You can slowly sip and savor this chocolate masterpiece inside their beautiful dining room. Or you can get a cup to go for 4.90 Euros like I did one cold and gris Paris afternoon.

As I strolled along the scenic Seine admiring the bridges (ponts) and architecture, I made sweet love to my chocolat chaud. Forget about all those silly women's magazine articles that say sex is better than chocolate. After one sip of this heavenly chocolate concoction, you'll agree that chocolate is the best!! Passersby smiled as they watched me lustfully sipping away while they quickly consulted Google Maps for Angelina's address. Although you might be tempted to pair it with something sweet or chocolatey from the shop, don't you dare! It tastes best sipped solo or with a warm, flaky, and plain buttery croissant. Now that's what I call a cup of hot chocolate!! **Bon appétit!!** *(November 2017)*

FRANCE & ITALY

Both Countries do Cheese & Wine so Well

I'm delighted anytime I can meet up with Edouard, an old friend, and a real Parisian monsieur. I met him more than 30 years ago when he and his family hosted Catherine, his relative and my friend, when we were backpacking through Europe. His father, Kalouste, was a retired tailor who lived in the Parisian suburb of Bois-Colombes. He was so kind to us and taught us so much about French & Parisian life.

Unfortunately, it isn't possible to meet up with Kalouste anymore, but it is always so nice to rendezvous with Edouard. Most people think that making love or sex are involved in a rendezvous, but a rendezvous is any type of meeting.

Anyway, on one rendezvous in Paris between bites of steak frites and sips of red wine, I went on and on about how the French did everything so well. The wine. The cheese. The wine & the cheese. The baguettes. The macarons. The croissants. Fashion. Eau de Parfum. The French nose knows.

I noticed that Edouard did not stop me from complimenting the French on everything they exceled at. He just smiled and constantly nodded in full agreement like a proud Frenchie. C'est magnifique!

Now don't get me wrong, London's an awesome city otherwise Britain wouldn't be called Great Britain, but Paris is Paris. It is the bee's knees!! It just is! No ifs ands or buts!

He agreed that the Italians were experts in making cheese, wine, and clothing, too. On the Eurostar from Gare du Nord to London's St. Pancras the next morning; I felt a bit sad as the train headed to Grey Britain. I tried to look on the bright side and thought of nice things waiting for me back in the UK like fish & chips, short bread, biscuits (bickies), and Marmite. The English do produce some good cheeses like Wensleydale, Stilton, and Cheddar. Kent is quickly becoming known for its vineyards. As far as fashion goes, the British have produced luxury labels such as Anya Hindmarch, Burberry, Smythson of Bond Street, Stella McCartney, and Victoria Beckham, etc. They make Bentleys, Jaguars, and Land Rovers, too. Lest not forget, Wallace & Gromit, The Beatles, and Tim Berners-Lee of the World Wide Web. Thanks UK!

However, France is France!!!! "Vive la France!!"

Voila!!

GERMANY

Frankfurt

The Würste Wheel

Germany's famous Christmas markets have always been the talk of the town so that was my first stop when I arrived in Frankfurt.

As I strolled around the festive market with its decorative wooden huts selling crafts, food & drink, I noticed a big crowd gathered around a booth. Not wanting to experience any FOMO, I made a beeline for it.

What I ended up seeing was the worst würste wheel. Vegetarians and vegans would be horrified by its presence. However, to a würste lover, it would most likely be the best of the würste.

Hefty German men with sausage like fingers turned sausage links and rings in all different shapes and sizes & countless types of würste on a huge silver iron wheel that swung in mid-air. The makeshift stove was fired underneath by a red-hot eternal flame. There was Bockwurst, Bratwurst, Knackwurst, Kochwurst, Liverwurst, and Weisswurst. Very excited locals and tourists easily parted ways with their Euros for a bit of sausage before heading off to the beer hut for something to wash it all down with. I, on the other hand, headed to the Bavarian pretzel kiosk for a warm, chubby, and doughy soft pretzel knot with a sprinkle of salt on top before seeking out a glass of Riesling wine.

Last December, I found myself in the pink city of Toulouse, France. Since it was "Tis the season," I sought out the Christmas market held at Place du Capitole. It did not disappoint. Just as the Germans were excited about their beer and würste; I was excited about all things French. How could you resist hot red wine, crêpes, beignets, and thick slices of French bread with melted cheese and Armagnac? Yummy! Bon appétit!

Two years later, I went to Hyde Park Winter Wonderland in London where there was a similar würste wheel and some Bavarian beer stalls and halls. Once again, I rejected all types of sausages and bought a huge cinnamon roll which I nibbled on while merrily strolling around taking in all the lights and Christmas decorations. Eater beware tip: It might be best to eat after you've gone on a few amusement park rides, dontcha think?

(December 2014-Toulouse, France, December 2015-Frankfurt, Germany & December 2017-London, England)

GREECE

Greek Sweets, Greek Food & Greek Drinks

Expect to see these foods on a taverna or bakery menu or for sale on Greece's streets.

Greek Sweets:

Amygdaloto, Bougatsa, Fystiki, Galaktoboureko, Kourabiedes, Loukoumades, Pasteli, Yiaourti me Meli, and Loukoumi (Greek Turkish Delight) with flavors such as rosewater, lemon, and mastic. And finally, Baklava and Kataifi!

Greek Food:

Choriatiki, Dakos, Dolmadakia, Fava, Feta, Gyros, Koulouri, Moussaka, Pastitsio, Saganaki, Skordalia, Spanakopita, Souvlaki, Taramasalata, Tzatziki, and Yemista. Enjoy!

Drinking in Greece:

Ouzo, Tsipouro, Mastika, Raki, and Retsina. In fact, Greece has (PDO) Protected Designation of Origin status for ouzo. Yamas! Cheers!

Athens

Fighting over Sardines at Lunch

Little did I know when I asked a staff member at the City Circus Athens Hostel for a calamari recommendation, that it would lead to a foodie encounter of the weirdest kind. He told me about a taverna that was around a 5-minute walk away that served authentic food and a fresh catch of the day, but he couldn't remember its name. He explained that the chef was getting older, so it might be open for lunch only. He Googled the restaurant somehow, found it online, and showed me a picture of it. It was near the market and you needed to walk down into it, as it was in an underground basement. I thanked him and excitedly and hungrily set off for it.

Minutes later, I passed by the market he had mentioned where vendors sold everything from pink salt, baklava, loukoumi (Greek Turkish Delight), and olives, etc. I had never seen so many black, green, mixed, and Kalamata olives in my life! There were overflowing buckets of olives soaking in olive oil everywhere. I have seen many baskets of dried olives in Fez, Morocco, and olives for sale at markets in Italy and France but not to this extent. How could one olive vendor compete with another? I tried to figure out what the USP (unique selling point) could be other than their color but struggled to come up with one.

I wasn't in the market for olives or olive oil right then and there, but my sweet tooth was seduced by some pale pink chubby cubes of rose loukoumi. I bought a few pieces and continued my hunt for the restaurant with no known name. About one minute later, I noticed a building across the street on the corner that had a stairwell and worn and graffitied brown doors that were flung wide open. The street sign read Theatrou. I made a beeline for it. Could this be the place?

Once there, I peered inside and down under. It seemed busy and lively. This must be the place. I quickly climbed down the stairs and found the rustic looking dining room to be plain and casual. It was filled with dark-haired Greeks with olive-colored skin. How I envy them for their sunny and warm Mediterranean climate. I stood out like a sore thumb and as a tourist with my fair skin and dark ash blond hair.

A young Greek waiter pointed out a table for me to sit at. I bet he was either a Christos, Demitri, Ioannis, Nico, or Yorgos. About a minute later, he approached my table and set it with a placemat and a napkin. He gave me a white plate with a huge chunk of bread on it and then he left. The chef/owner who had just appeared on the scene went over to one of the large pots on the old stove and ladled something onto a plate. He came over to my table, smiled at me, and put down a plate of sautéed sardines. As I looked at the fish in their silvery glistening skins, I had a hard time smiling back at him, as I hate sardines. I absolutely hate them!! I was dreaming of eating sautéed fresh calamari in olive oil, lemon, and garlic or fried squid. I hate sardines!! I don't care if I miss the Sardine Festival in Lisbon in June!

I tried to explain to the chef that I didn't like sardines but was unsuccessful. It was a very lost in translation moment. He abruptly left my table in an annoyed and frustrated mood. I've really done it now, I thought, as I felt all eyes in the dining room on me. My waiter returned to my table about 30 seconds later. I tried to explain to him that I don't eat sardines. I just do not eat them, no ifs ands or buts. However, if they were the only thing left to eat on this earth, then maybe I'd have no choice and just eat them. I'm afraid I struck out a second time. The waiter left and went over to talk to the chef.

The very upset chef came over to my table and left with the untouched plate of sardines. He loudly yelled something causing all diners to look and stare at me again. I wanted to crawl under the table and stay there until closing, but if I did that, I would miss out on sightseeing in Athens. I sat in my chair frozen and confused. The chef went back and took his place in the front of the restaurant behind his cooking station where he stirred and stirred some mystery concoction in his huge pot.

I turned every shade of pink and red found on a PMS color chart. A few minutes later, the waiter came back to my table with a bowl of beige colored soup. Boring! However, I was thrilled that it wasn't sardines. Halfway through my tasty chickpea soupy stew, the chef approached my table again. He held a framed photo of Francis Ford Coppola, the famous movie director and wine maker, which he gave me to inspect. "American?" he asked in a thick Greek accent as he pointed at Francis and then at me. He paused for a moment waiting for my response or reaction. I nodded my head to confirm my American status. This caused him to wildly shake his head and the rest of his body in excitement. You would've thought I told him that Francis was my father. This made me think of my father who had died the year before after a long, sad, and painful struggle with Alzheimer's disease

The satisfied and very happy chef left. I caught my waiter's eye. He came over to my table and I asked him for my check. He said no. He went back to the cooking station where he spoke with the chef. He came back to my table and refused the Euros that I held out to him. The chef went to the opposite end of the taverna. I walked over there to thank him and say goodbye. He picked up Francis's photo again and when I went to take his picture, he gave both of us a copper cup which we clanged together in celebration. Everyone in the taverna laughed and smiled. Talk about a lunchtime Greek drama full of tragedy & comedy!

This was one of the most bizarre eating experiences that I've had on the road so far. I would've loved to have had one of those Greek salads that passed by me, but due to its all being Greek to me it just was not possible, even though I did point one out to my waiter. Pointing at something is not necessarily the same thing as verbally ordering it I learned that day.

I left in search of a taverna for a shot of ouzo, raki, or mastika just as two Greek guys started playing some music on ancient looking Greek guitars. The taverna might have been Diporto. If I ever bump into Francis in Napa in the future, I must tell him how much this Greek chef loves him. I've been to Buenos Aires, but if I ever go back, I would like to stay at Be Jardín Escondido by Coppola which looks lovely. Yamas!

(November 2016)

Crete-Rethymno
The Phyllo Dough Maker and His Wife

Late one afternoon, I stumbled upon a real live phyllo/filo pastry maker, Giorgos H, in Rethymno on the Greek island of Crete. Yes, some things are still crafted by hand in this age of automation and robots. If you're Greek or live in Greece, phyllo is a kitchen staple.

Once inside, I met Giorgos and his sweet wife, Katerina. They gave me a tour of their simple old school, yet highly productive kitchen/factory. Primitive tools and burlap supplies decorated its interior. The real magic and action happened on the huge tables where the ultra-thin phyllo is rolled out, stretched, and dried. Giorgos makes kataifi, thin-strand pastry, too. For the past 60+ years, he's worked hard making dough which Katerina bakes sweet Greek specialties from.

Since they didn't speak English and I don't speak any Greek, we communicated via universal body language/emotions. Katerina escorted me to a seat in the back of the store/workshop. When I asked what type of trees were in the garden, she went and picked a piece of fruit from one. It was a pomegranate, just ripe for the picking. She immediately cut it in half and offered me a piece. It was meant for sharing between strangers who were now friends. The Greeks excel in being hospitable and truly practice philoxenia.

We sat for a few minutes eating, smiling at each other, resting, laughing, and just enjoying the moment. It was a lovely break from a busy day! About 30 minutes later, I got up to leave, but not before buying some syrupy, sweet, and nutty baklava. Katerina tried to tell me something, but I didn't understand her. Fortunately, an English-speaking customer came in to buy some pastry and acted as a translator. She told me to come back the next day around 10:30 AM to see the phyllo demo. I thanked her for this valuable information. I asked what she was making with her phyllo dough and she told me Spanakopita (spinach and feta cheese pie).

The next morning at 10:30 AM, I arrived at the phyllo factory/shop at 30 Manouil Vernardou Street, about a 10-minute walk from the Rimondi Fountain in Old Town. Giorgos danced and spoke to the phyllo as he rolled it out while everyone including his wife and son watched. It was live food theater! My visit ended on a sweet note, as I bought some very fresh kataifi rolls.

(November 2017)

Kea (Cyclades)
Aristaios, Greek Grocery Store

The foodie and seeker of "local life" found me on an endless walk from my hotel in Korissia to Mylopotamos. I'd already done 10,000 steps that morning, so had met my daily step goal. I now felt a bit lost, dazed, and confused. And a bit hot and tired from the very sunny Mediterranean sun. It was time to ask for directions to Aristaios, experiential farm, so I stopped at a local restaurant. Luck was on my side, as I ended up meeting the owner's charming Greek family.

His brother showed me their garden area where food was casually served amidst orangey orange trees. He gave me a quick tour of the Folklore Museum with its many antiquated Greek artifacts, too.

We headed back to the restaurant where I met his sweet and spicy mother, Maria Mouzaki-Chionatou. On hearing that I was a writer, Maria became very excited and with her son's help, explained to me that she had written a few books about Kea. Unfortunately, they were written in Greek. She insisted on giving me one with some English words as a gift. The Greeks have hospitality in their blood, no matter how little or big the gift. I was touched by her gift and generosity. The thin book, "The Journey of Krithinitis," (Bread of Barley) had beautiful and detailed charcoal pencil illustrations. To top it off, she poured me a shot glass of Mavroudi wine, winked at me, and laughed as I quickly drank it. She enjoyed seeing me appreciate her gift and I enjoyed receiving it even though it was a bit too early to drink. However, being on vacation and being kind requires one to break habits and protocols! Those Greeks and their hospitality! You've got to love them! I am sure Zeus Xenios would be proud of Maria. Yamas! Cheers!

The adventure continued when her son drove me to Aristaios, their nearby store. Aristaios was the God of many food making items such as beekeeping, olive growing, and cheesemaking. A sign listed all the store's products in Greek. Aristaios is a one stop shopping source on the island for organic food, fresh fruits & veggies, olive oil, sundried tomatoes, capers & caper leaves, olives, cookies, liqueurs, jams, nougat, pasta, sesame bars, honey, and olive oil soap. It could easily give any gourmet food store a run for their money!

If you're looking for a Greek island not far from Athens and about 70 minutes via ferry from Lavrio, head to Kea where the Greeks go, unlike other islands which swell with more tourists than locals.
(October 2017)

GREECE & POLAND

Kind of Like a Bagel: Greece's Koulouri & Poland's Obwarzanek Krakowski

I first saw the Koulouri in Greece's second city, Thessaloniki, and a few days later in Athens. A few street food vendors sold these sesame seed bread rings, Koulouri, from rickety wooden carts for about half a Euro.

The best time to eat one is in the early AM when they're fresh, warm, moist, soft, and instantly melt in your mouth. I gobbled one down at 5 AM not giving it any time to get hard. For once, I didn't complain about having to catch an early morning train.

A few days later in Kraków, Poland, I saw vendors selling similar bread rings coated with poppy seeds or sesame seeds. In Poland, this pretzel/bagel concoction is called the Obwarzanek Krakowski. I guess you could say the Poles and Greeks are kind of eating the same thing with a different name.

These round doughy bread rings made me a bit homesick for a chubby bagel from H & H Bagels, Murray's Bagels, or Pick a Bagel which I used to nosh on a lot when I lived in the Big Apple.

(October 2016/November 2016)

IRELAND

Growing Up Irish & St. Patrick's Day

Unfortunately, oysters and Guinness were not on the menu or on the table on St. Patrick's Day. Every year on March 17th, the green holiday rolled around and every year the same holiday fare of ham & cabbage with boiled & buttery potatoes was served. Some years corned beef was served for a change of food scenery. For dessert, there was Irish Soda Bread with or without raisins. The adults at the adult table meaning my parents, maternal grandparents, aunts, and uncles had Irish Coffee. Unfortunately, the kids at the kids table which consisted of siblings and cousins, were not eligible to enjoy this hot Irish whiskey drink.

I can't that I was bowled over by the traditional and festive Irish fare, but I can say it was nice to be surrounded by my family and friends. Erin Go Bragh!

On past trips to Ireland, it was in Dublin where I enjoyed a pint of Guinness and in Galway Bay where I indulged in very fresh from the sea oysters.

dodublin.ie

ITALY

Milan

Live Coffee Theater

If someone told me that I would see good live theater in Milan; I would have corrected them and told them that they must mean opera, right? At La Scala. Afterall, everyone knows that NYC's Broadway and London are the best places to see theater & theatre.

When it comes to coffee, the Italians know how to make a good cup. So, when in Milan, I headed to Piazza Cordusio to see live coffee theater. Or rather, I went to Starbucks Reserve Roastery (starbucksreserve.com) near the Duomo. So very convenient for tourists. I think they planned it that way, don't you?

In 2018, the coffee giant arrived in Milano with a bang. I arrived a bit later with no bang. As soon as I opened the door, I felt like I had arrived in a spacious two-level "Coffee Land" which was half theater and half amusement park. The word flamboyant came to mind more than once. Coffee beans swirled around, besides, and above me before they were ground, pressed, slow-brewed, and crafted into some coffee concoction or other. The resulting brown liquid was poured into coffee cups or infused in some type of coffee cocktail at the upper-level bar. The excitement continued over at the affogato station where ice cream was created with liquid nitrogen. I was tempted more by the Princi® pastries and pizzas, as I don't really drink coffee. Although, I love the smell of other people's coffee or a coffee body scrub.

For a live viewing of the bean to cup process or to use the cool bathroom, that is, if you make a pricey purchase, come here. If you're seeking a cup of joe and need to catch a train from Milano Centrale, the coffee at the McCafé in the train station will do, plus there's free Wi-Fi.

Arrivederci.

(October 2018)

Milan Travel Tips:
welcometomilano.it
milanolovesyou.com

ITALY & GREECE

Drinking Coffee in Italy and Greece

After observing how Italians & Greeks drink their coffee, I arrived at these potential conclusions: The Italians stand while drinking their cappuccino or espresso while the Greeks sit and linger over their single, double, triple espressos, or Ellinikos Kafes (Greek coffees). The Italians are known for being good fashion designers, so timing is crucial, but so is la dolce vita, so they enjoy a quick cup before scooting off on their stylish and colorful Vespa scooter somewhere favoloso. Ciao! I'm not sure if the Greeks linger over their coffee because they're busy discussing Greece's economy and wanting to get their Euro's worth, or if it's just their philosophical nature?

I'm always amazed when I feel rushed out of an empty place. This never or rarely happens in Greece as a café or taverna owner is born understanding the concept & importance of hospitality. Wouldn't an owner or a manager want their place to be busy inside, outside, and have a line? Don't crowds bring people? Years ago, when I lived in NYC's Gramercy Park, there was always a line outside of Friend of a Farmer on the weekend, but after enjoying its Vermont like breakfasts, I understood why. It was worth the wait!

MALTA

Pastizz & Pastizzi

The best way to describe the Maltese pastizz is to compare it to other same but different handheld international foods. It's kind of sort of like but not quite like a British pasty, a Chinese egg roll/spring roll, a Greek tiropita, kreatopita, or kalitsounia, an Indian samosa, an Italian panzerotto or calzone, a Moroccan briouat, or a Spanish & Portuguese empanada, etcetera. Almost the same but different!!

A local in Valletta told me about them when I asked for directions to St. John's Co-Cathedral. He mentioned this pastry was great for a hangover. He didn't actually say hangover. He said they were great to eat on a Saturday or Sunday morning after a late night out. He mentioned they were cheap, too. And cheap they were, all over town & the islands of Gozo and Comino! I paid 90 centimes to 1 Euro for a small cup of tea and a chickpea pastizz. You can get them with a ricotta cheese filling, too. The one I had at the posh Caffe Cordina in Valletta cost a little bit more, but you're paying to eat it in a lovely Maltese venue.

vistitmalta.com
heritagemalta.org

POLAND

Kraków
Eating Pierogi with the Local Gals

My father was Polish which makes me half Polish so on my first night in Kraków; I felt I owed it to the 50% Pole in me and to my hungry stomach to seek out a pierogi joint.

Pierogi are like Chinese dumplings, Italian ravioli, and Japanese gyoza. If you eat one you ate a pierog. If you eat two, then you ate pierogi. The Poles stuff them with all sorts of fillings such as potato, cheese, onions, cherries, spinach, mushrooms, cabbage, sauerkraut, meat, whatever the chef might fancy, or whatever is available.

Lucky for me, I didn't have to stroll too far from the city center before I stumbled upon Kuchnia Staropolska U Babci Maliny on ul. Szpitalna 38.

Once inside, the cozy and woody interior was inviting yet a bit creepy with its dim lighting and strange decor. I felt like I was in an odd relative's house or in a funhouse with weird and wonderful stuff to purposely amuse and shock visitors. I was determined to escape these rooms after I had gotten my fill of Polish dumplings.

The majority of standing in line or seated and eating diners were blond-haired or blond highlighted females from Poland or somewhere in Eastern Europe. It was nice to feel like I kind of belonged with my Polish background and highlighted blond hair. Unfortunately, I do not speak Polish and honestly do not know if I will ever find the time to learn. Although, I do know a few words. Chleb means bread, ser means cheese, and ziemniaki means potatoes.

I browsed at all the different food items listed on the wall mounted menu while I waited to order. It would be potato, cheese, and onion pierogi for me and a glass of white wine. When it came time to order, the cashier didn't fully understand my order and I did not understand a word she said. It was a lost in translation moment. I quickly resorted to performing universal sign/body language. She gave me a menu and I pointed to the items that I wanted to order. I slowly said, "fried," and she seemed a bit confused. I tried to motion the concept of sautéed via haphazard hand signals. She looked at me and said, "Ruskie." I had no idea what she meant but thought it best to nod and just eat what I was given. In the worst case, I could stomach something like sauerkraut. I paid, got my glass of wine and a ticket with 47 scrawled on it.

I proceeded upstairs to a crowded dining room filled with gals of all ages, shapes, and sizes. I felt like I had just walked into a girls' night or hen night/bachelorette party. They all turned to stare at me as I sat down on a long wooden bench. From time to time, I felt them staring at me, so I just smiled back as I waited for my dumplings. They laughed, ate, and drank while I hungrily waited. I'm not sure if they were laughing at me, but they were having a grand old time. About 15 minutes later, 47 came up, so I went downstairs to retrieve my doughy dumplings. I gave my ticket to the lady in the kitchen and received a plate of lightly sautéed "Ruskie" pierogi. They looked like what I wanted. I was too hungry to turn down anything at this point.

I went back upstairs where I dug into my pierogi and felt all eyes on me as I took my first bite. The dozen plump pan-fried dumplings were bursting with a fluffy and tasty cheese, potato, and onion filling. They met my approval and I think the gals approved of my approval. I flashed them a big smile as I departed. I will fondly remember that meal with the Polish gals. I only wish I could tell my Polish father about my pierogi adventure. **Smacznego!**

(November 2016)

The Polish Milk Bar

The Milk Bar or bar mleczny was an important part of Poland's past both before and after wars. These plain as can be historical cafeterias served Poles very basic and traditional Polish food like pierogi as well as dairy based foods. Check out either Bar Mleczny Centrum and Pod Temidą in Kraków, for an authentic and reasonably priced dining experience.

The Polish milk bars are a bit different than Milk Bar shops (milkbarstore.com) in the USA which sell cookies, pies, and cakes.

Polish Cuisine

The Poles eat a lot of cabbage, sausage, potatoes, mushrooms, and onions. Popular soups are beetrooty barszcz or sour rye soup. Bigos is a hearty meat and cabbage stew. Kielbasa is like a very long sausage. Naleśniki are pancake like crêpes.

Zapiekanka (Polish pizza) is a warm open-faced baguette with cheese, mushrooms, and ketchup that can be bought on the street or at kiosks in train stations. Placki are potato pancakes. It might be a good idea to eat either before drinking some vodka?

PORTUGAL

Port, Custard Tarts, Sardines & Cod

If you love port wine, a trip to the Douro Valley is a must. If you've ever wanted to crush grapes with your feet, September-October is the best time to go. You might even see some boats transporting wine down the river. In 2001, my first port of call in Lisbon was at the Port Wines Institute where I slowly sipped a 40-years old port for about $7. I was 33 years old which made that port 7 years older than me!

If you have a sweet tooth, the creamy custard tart Pastel de nata/Pastéis de nata (Portuguese Custard Tart/Tarts)can be found in pastelarias all over. Don't worry if the tart's top has a few burnt marks on it, as it adds to its flavor.

If you're a sardine lover, Lisbon has a Sardine Festival in June that's tied in with Saint Anthony's Day. Or you can always go to The Fantastic World of Portuguese Sardines in Porto & Lisboa, where you can buy colorful tin cans of the slippery silvery fish.

Cod is all over and can be eaten a million ways. The important thing is to enjoy some bacalhau here.

visitportugal.com

SPAIN

Paella in Princeton & Madrid

I first tasted tapas in Princeton, NJ. On the way to meet a friend for them, I asked a man for directions to Mediterra **(mediterrarestaurant.com)**. Sensing his uncertainty, I quickly added the word tapas to my inquiry. He told me that he didn't know if there was a topless bar in town. This caused me to blush a little. This journey was beginning to feel just as important and interesting as the destination. Fortunately, the next person I asked knew exactly where the restaurant was located. Between sips of red wine and bites of a lovely chicken and seafood paella, the travel tale was shared in much the same way I am telling it here.

Years later, on a trip to Madrid, I ate some paella for lunch, as I was told that only tourists eat it for dinner. Who wants to look like a tourist? Madrileños tend to eat a heavy lunch (el almuerzo) around 2 PM and a light dinner (la cena) around 9 PM or later. And let us not forget about the tapas (Spanish snacks) such as Iberian ham, olives, and calamari, etc. which are nibbled on after work or in the early/late evening.

spain.info

SLOVENIA

Lake Bled
Bled Cream Cake

The bus from Ljubljana took about 1-1/2 hours to get to Bled in the scenic Julian Alps. Once in town, I quickly found out that Bled Cream Cake was this little Slovenian town's star dessert.

I enjoyed a slice of creamy Kremšnita after a trip to Bled Castle and Island via a pletna boat with a colorful striped awning. The day had been chilly, yet sunny, which caused the castle to be reflected in the lake. Beautiful! Absolutely, beautiful! On the ride over, I was told that different places made the cake the same way, but a little bit different. I wasn't sure if this was true or just said to sell two slices but supporting the local economy when on the road is important. Plus, I was curious, so I found myself trying two different cake slices. The vanilla custard flavor was similar in both, but one might have had a wee bit more rum. If the cake weren't so creamy it would make a great "gift from trip" for friends & family.

(November 2018)

bled.si

NORTH AFRICA

MOROCCO

Fez

A Slow-Cooked Tagine at Café Clock

After a morning spent walking around in circles while trying to navigate the labyrinthine of winding streets, city walls, and narrow alleyways of Fez's Medina, it was time to admit defeat. We had bobbed and weaved our way around tons and tons of shops and stalls selling kebabs, colorful leather pointed toe babouche slippers, bags, belts, stacks and stacks of clay tagine pots, camel heads, baskets overflowing with dried black olives, and many slowpoke donkeys in the process.

We were officially lost! Lost! It was now time to accept help from the very same teenage boy whose help we had rejected an hour earlier. We were going nowhere fast and getting hungrier with every stroke of the clock. Desperate attempts to find Café Clock and its tagines on our own had failed.

Fortunately, we bumped into the boy again and readily accepted his help, for what seemed like a reasonable number of Moroccan dirhams (MAD). He led as we followed and then he walked behind us, but he never walked with us which seemed a bit odd.

Later, I asked him about it, and he told us that he did that because he wasn't a licensed tour guide.

Our unofficial tour guide knew the general area where Café Clock was located, but he still got a bit lost. This made us feel a bit better and not like total losers. We finally found Café Clock at 7 Derb el Magana when we looked up and saw its tall clock and bells. Eureka!! The restaurant's name now made sense! If lost, always look up, as you just might find it using this method!

Although it was early November, it was warm enough to dine up on the roof terrace. Once seated, a chicken tagine couldn't be ordered fast enough. However, the joke was on us when the waiter said it would take about an hour. Good things or in this case, a tasty tagine, would be worth waiting for.

In the meantime, we quenched our thirst with a fresh mint lemonade and a beetroot juice while we involuntarily and hungrily waited. An hour later, good things came to us who had waited. The cone shaped lid of the terracotta tagine pot was lifted to reveal a stew with a spicy fragrant odor. The tagine didn't disappoint with its mélange of ingredients such as ginger, turmeric, garlic, preserved lemons, and green olives. It would've been the bee's knees if the chicken had more time to get a bit moister.

The adventurous young male backpacker seated next to us ordered a camel burger. He passed the time writing away. He'd have bragging rights for his bravery if his stomach made it out of there alive, I thought. In the worst case, his journal contained all the details.

When we finished about 1-3/4 hours later, we found our unofficial officially ours tour guide waiting for us outside the café. We felt relieved as not even a mouse could find the cheese in this maze of a walled city. He told us he'd waited for us for some reason or another. I thought we'd agreed for him to come back an hour or so later, but obviously something had been lost in translation. We didn't really know where he was while we were eating, but we took his word for it. This meant that his meter had been running from the time he started secretly escorting us until now and would end when we were back at our riad, Dar Fes Medina. We headed back not saying much as he led the way and then kind of led the way. As a bit expected, he took advantage of our dazed and confused state by hiking up the price a few more MAD's which made me a bit MAD. Desperate times call for desperate measures! I was just glad that we'd made it back to our home sweet riad. Hopefully, there'd be some Moroccan mint tea waiting for us in the room with the pretty, colorful, intricate & memorable mosaic floor!
(November 2016)

Fez Tip: Café Clock **(cafeclock.com)** offers cooking classes for foodies and aspiring cooks who want to learn how to prepare all kinds of tagines.

Types of B'stellas:
B'stella b l'hout (Fish Bastilla)
B'stella b'djaj (Chicken Bastilla)

Types of Tagines:
Tagine b l'hout (Fish Tagine)
Tagine djaj Mqalli (Chicken Tagine with preserved lemons and olives)
Tagine b l'khodra (Seasonal Vegetables Tagine)
Tagine b t'mer w l'berkok (Tagine with Prune & Date)

And finally, Dessert:
Blighat b t'mer (Date and Pastry Rolls)

Moroccan Mint Tea

The manager and lovely staff at Dar Fes Medina, the charming riad where we stayed in Fez, served some lovely Moroccan mint tea upon arrival, at breakfast, and before our departure.

The informal tea like ceremony involved the mint tea being poured from a teapot with a very long, thin, and curvy spout about 12 inches away from our glasses. It was an up in the air pour that created a bit of excitement as well as a froth on top. The tea pourers always poured the perfect pour! I know I could never pull it off without spilling it all over or burning myself with the scalding hot tea in the process. Practice makes perfect! I will need a lot of practice!

When I asked how the tea was prepared, I was told that sugar and spearmint leaves were added to the mint green tea. The British take their tea and theatre very seriously, but it's the Moroccans who perform live tea theater. One sip of this tea will calm your nerves from a day spent in the hectic medina or at the souk where you'll bargain over colorful slippers, purses, or small tea glasses as you try to navigate the walled city and avoid crashing into stacked stacks of clay tagine pots & lids. And dodge donkeys while you hear & scream, "Balak! Balak!"   *(November 2016)*

NORDICA & SCANDINAVIA

ICELAND

Reykjavík
White Russians at the Lebowski Bar

Burgers, bowling lane decor, a jukebox, cool bar stools, milkshakes, and 20 or so types of White Russians are on offer at the Lebowski Bar (**lebowskibar.is**). It's a little bit of retro Hollywood in the land of fire & ice on 20a Laugavegur Street. Drinking and dining is not cheap in Iceland, so be sure to visit during Happy Hour from 4-7 PM.

Reykjavík

Happy Hour Guide

Drinking in Iceland is not cheap, but you can find a happy hour somewhere from Noon to 11 PM.

Tip: Download the free **Reykjavík Grapevine Happy Hour app-Appy Hour (grapevine.is)**.

Some happy hours are every day. Some go from Noon to 7 PM, 2 PM-5 PM, 2 PM-6 PM, 2 PM-9 PM, 3 PM-6 PM, 3 PM-7 PM, 3 PM-8 PM, 4 PM-6 PM,4 PM-6:30 PM, 4 PM-7 PM, 4 PM-8 PM, 5 PM-6 PM, 5 PM-6:30 PM, 5 PM-7 PM, 5 PM-8 PM, 9 PM- 11 PM, and 9:30 PM-10:30 PM.

Cheers!

SWEDEN

South of Stockholm
Swedish Meatballs at IKEA

After watching the Swedish Changing of the Guard which starts promptly at 12:15 PM (Sundays at 1:15 PM) and seeing all sorts of modern & contemporary art at Moderna Museet, both of which were free to see (Fee for special art exhibitions), I had worked up an appetite. The tons of ads for Swedish meatballs scattered all over Stockholm didn't help at all and made me hungrier by the minute. So, what did I do? I headed to IKEA. Yes, IKEA.

I had first tasted the little meatballs at IKEA in Plymouth Meeting, PA (a Philly suburb) which was their first USA store in 1985. My family lives about 30 minutes from there and after my father ate them, he got us all hooked on them. He liked their taste and their price.

After admiring some subway art and design, I jumped on the metro from T-CENTRALEN to Skärholmen which took about 25 minutes, caught bus # 173 from the station which took 10 minutes, and finally arrived at Sweden's largest IKEA store in Kungens Kurva.

Once inside, I felt like I was at my local IKEA. The only difference was that most shoppers were Swedes speaking Swedish which confirmed that I was far from home. I had worked up an appetite in transit, so headed straight to the café and ordered my meatballs. For 29 SEK or about 2.50 GBP, I was served 8 small meatballs, 3 boiled potatoes, gravy, lingonberries, and peas. Lingonberries are rich in antioxidants and are kind of like cranberries. The meal fit the bill for authentic and wallet friendly Swedish fare. They made me think of my deceased father. I love and miss him. That's the thing about food, it has the power to create and keep all kinds of memories alive for years to come.

Before I left the huge store, I bought a bag of black licorice as flat pack furniture was not on my shopping list that day. I was on my way to Bangkok the next day via Norwegian and wanted to pick up a tasty plane snack. I stopped bringing protein rich nuts years ago as I had a few flights where fellow passengers with nut allergies forced me to involuntarily refrain from snacking on them. Have you ever heard of anything so nutty? In the past, I have been mad as heck after hearing such requests especially after I had shelled out a lot for nuts. I only bring safe snacks now. *(May 2017)*

stockholm.com

South of Stockholm

Fika at IKEA

We all take one. The coffee break, that is. The Swedes fika or have a fikapaus at least two times a day. The rest of us have some sort of coffee or tea break. It's basically a chance for all of us to hit the pause button during the day and relax for a few minutes.

Before I left IKEA around 3:30 PM on a Saturday afternoon, I decided to fika with the Swedes for a truly Swedish experience at an iconic Swedish store.

To fully experience a Swedish fika, I ordered a sugary and spicy cinnamon roll with my cup of tea. My IKEA fika cost 5 SEK for a cup of tea with no lid and 5 SEK for a cinnamon roll (kanelbulle) for a grand total of only 10 SEK. There are many cozy cafes in Stockholm to fika at, but you will pay a bit more Kronas.   *(May 2017)*

I hope you enjoy your afternoon coffee whether it's on a coffee break in a break room, a fika in a fikarum or in a cosy kaffehörna (coffee corner) at home! Everyone deserves a break!

visitstockholm.com

Stockholm
The Lakrits Street Vendor

The Swedes love Swedish fish, but they really love licorice (lakrits), too. They even eat salty lakrits. It's an acquired taste!

On a sunny spring day, I passed a lakrits street vendor on my way to ABBA The Museum (abbathemuseum.com). I felt like a kid in an outside candy store! I'm not sure how many inches a lakrits strand was, but it looked longer and thicker than a shoelace. Hopefully, it tasted better. After much consideration and temptation, I chose a salty black strand from all the colorful strands in flavors such as bubblegum, cherry, lemon, pear, strawberry, and Tutti Frutti for 25 SEK. Worth it!   *(May 2015)*

All Sorts of Lakkrís, Liquorice, and Licorice:
This licorice encounter made me think of the Icelanders and their love of black licorice (lakkrís), chocolate lakkrís, and salty black lakkrís. The British love all sorts of liquorice especially round, square, or chubby multi-coloured liquorice allsorts.

All sorts of licorice for all sorts of sweet tooths!

CENTRAL & SOUTH AMERICA

ARGENTINA

Buenos Aires

pickupthefork.com

Pick Up The Fork (pickupthefork.com) has got to be one of the best names for a foodie website. The worst thing is putting down the fork. Thank goodness you can eat empanadas with your hands.

Buenos Aires

Steak

In between doing the tango, visiting Evita's grave, and attending a polo match, eating a cut of grass-fed beef is a must in BA, unless you're a vegetarian or vegan. After some bife at parrillas like Don Julio in Palermo Viejo or La Cabrera in Palermo, you'll agree that the gauchos are providing quality care for their cattle on the Pampas. Don't forget to try some ice cream! Unfortunately, I didn't know any Argentines to be invited to an asado, a social BBQ held in a friend or family member's backyard, but I have been a guest at some barbies down under which were quite tasty. I was told that the secret of a good asado comes from the quality of the meats, the coals, and the slow cooking process (2-4 hours). Don't forget the Malbec!

PANAMA

Panama City
Rum and Ceviche

There's no doubt that you'll work up an appetite after visiting the Panama Canal, the Biomuseo with its colorful exterior, and countless Panama hat stores.

And when you do feel any hunger pains coming on, take a trip to the Mercado de Mariscos. This fish market is loaded with seafood & fish vendors along with several nearby restaurants that sell all types of fish dishes and ceviche. Or perhaps get an enchilada and some tostones (fried green plantains).

An ideal place to wet your whistle with some type of rum infused cocktail while you watch the sunset from its rooftop is at Casa Casco in the cobblestoned streets of the Old Quarter or Casco Viejo.

When I left Panama for Atlantic City, NJ via a stop in FL, a hurricane was doing its stuff there before it headed to the Isthmus of Panama. The only hurricane I wanted to experience was a drinkable one.

(October 2018)

UK (ENGLAND)

The Full English Breakfast

After living in the UK for almost a decade, I'm convinced that the English like things in FULL, such as the Full Monty and the Full English Breakfast.

The Full English Breakfast (brekkie) will always satisfy a hungry person and shock a dieter. A tourist will welcome the big brekkie as it will set them up nicely with energy for the rest of the day. Calories can be burned while sightseeing or out on a ramble.

Americans would probably compare the Full English Breakfast to Denny's Grand Slam® breakfast. My father loved eating one before the start of a family road trip. **Good memories!**

The Full English breakfast fry-up consists of 8 varied ingredients: eggs, bacon, sausage, mushrooms, baked beans, grilled tomatoes, fried toast or toast, and black pudding. It has between 800-1,000 calories depending on how much bacon and sausage you eat. If you skip the baked beans or musical fruit, you might avoid any near future flatulence. The Half English Breakfast consists of eggs, bacon, tomato, toast, and mushrooms and is ideal for smaller appetites or dieters. The back bacon in the UK tastes like ham, so order streaky bacon if you want American bacon. **Rise and Shine! Good Morning!**

The Sunday Roast

The Sunday Roast in England can evoke similar cosy feelings like a hygge in Denmark does. In the winter, it's the perfect middle or end to a Sunday whether at home or in a pub. Hopefully, somewhere with a woody scented roaring fire. It's an ideal way to end a walk and feed an appetite after an afternoon ramble, too.

A Sunday roast can consist of roast beef, lamb, chicken, or pork with crispy crackling. Vegetables, roast potatoes, and light & airy Yorkshire Puddings with a dollop of rich gravy accompany it. Vegetarians can feast on a nut roast as it would be nutty to offer them anything else.

If you have room after your roast, you can indulge in one of many Afters (Desserts) such as Banoffee Pie, Crumble, English Trifle, Eton Mess, Figgy Pudding, Jam Roly-Poly, Knickerbocker Glory, Spotted Dick, Sticky Toffee Pudding, Syllabub, Treacle Tart, or Victoria Sponge Cake. Done and dusted!

I'm lucky to know a lovely British family who've invited me to many roasts at their home in Dulwich Village. Thanks Tim, Ann, Stewart, Jo & Tony!

Drinking Tea in England

Three minutes is ideal for letting your tea leaves or tea bag steep in jolly old England. It would be equivalent to the Italian concept of "al dente" for just right pasta in about 10 minutes. It's up to you whether you pour the tea or milk in first. Or have loose-leaf tea or tea bags. Decisions. Decisions.

The English indulge in afternoon tea between 3 PM - 5 PM. 4 PM is a popular time for tea. Scones, a variety of cakes, and finger sandwiches are served at an afternoon tea.

Cream Tea

A cream tea is much smaller than an afternoon tea. It consists of scones, hopefully, just baked scones, jam, cream, and a pot of tea. Jam is applied first followed by clotted cream at a Cornish (Cornwall) cream tea. At a Devon cream tea, clotted cream comes first followed by jam. If Borat Sagdiyev from the movie "Borat" was planning to take tea in the UK, he should take an etiquette course on the rules of taking tea, as well as a bathroom etiquette course, so he can act in a proper manner.

East London
A Bar in a Taxidermy Museum?

OMG!! You've got to see it to believe it! I'd visited the free **Grant Museum of Zoology** where I saw and expected to see skulls and brains. Even zoos have stuff like that, but dead stuff like that in bars?

I'd heard about the **Viktor Wynd Museum of Curiosities, Fine Art & Natural History** which piqued my curiosity, so one evening I headed over to the neighborhoods of Bethnal Green and Cambridge Heath. I entered the **Last Tuesday Society** (thelasttuesdaysociety.org) at 11 Mare Street shortly after 6:30 PM. I paid the admission fee and found myself in a dark bar with an odd décor, a few stuffed creatures, and some nook & cranny areas where guests could sip drinks in private.

It paid to be a Skinny Minny as I descended the very narrow gold staircase into a dungeon like area. I felt like I was in a taxidermy shop as I perused all sorts of bones and taxidermic creations. This haunted house like bar had some way-out stuff including a few erotic items. As I left this weird & wonderful bar 30 minutes later, I was glad I'd come and gotten an "eyeful."

(April 2017)

London
A Pharmacy in an Art Gallery?

Cool!! Confusing?? What was the artist trying to convey? These are probably some thoughts that might have crossed your mind when you cast your gaze on unique, inspiring, weird, and wonderful works of art. As a seeker of all things artsy, I got off the tube at Vauxhall and then walked 10 minutes to Damien Hirst's art collection gallery, the Newport Street Gallery (newportstreetgallery.com).

While many of us will not say what we think about most museum and gallery visits, I will. There's nothing better than art appreciation and immersing oneself in culture. It can be very relaxing and therapeutic. However, sometimes a museum/gallery headache can come over you after an hour or two and an exit might be necessary.

Since this is a small art gallery and not a huge museum, you probably won't get one. Plus, it has a pharmacy on site. I mean, a restaurant. Pharmacy 2 Café is a restaurant. A way cool one! The bar counter tops have all sorts of things in them and the bar stools are shaped like round pills. Now that's what I call a pharmacy! Free gallery entry.   *(Spring 2017)*

London

Biscuiteers really takes the biscuit!

Biscuits, biscuits, and more biscuits!

Biscuiteers (**biscuiteers.com**) located at 194 Kensington Park Road close to Notting Hill is a biscuits (bickies) emporium.

Every possible type of person, place, thing, occasion, or theme has been rolled out in biscuit form here. Animals, anniversary, après ski, baby boy, baby girl, baby shower, birds, birthdays, butterfly, cars, cats, champagne, congrats, dogs, engagement, fashion, first aid, flowers, fruit, get well, gin & tonic, happy, hug, I love you, love, new baby, new home, new job, safari, spa day, thank you, travel, weddings, and wine & cheese, etcetera, are all here waiting for you.

Hmm, now all you need is a nice cuppa tea to go along with that bickie. Fortunately, you're in the right country for one!

London

Borough Market is a Foodie's Paradise

After exiting the London Bridge underground station, stop. Stop looking down at your smartphone and look up to see the Shard (the unmissable tall pointy glass building). Then head on over to Borough Market food hall where you'll be spoiled for choice at this very old paradise for foodies! Paradise!! Paradise!!

It's an ideal culinary selfie spot with its diverse food stalls that sell everything from bread, calamari, charcuterie, cheese, fish & chips, fruits & veggies, paella, fresh seafood, and Thai food, etc.

(boroughmarket.org.uk)

Nearby Sightseeing Tips:
Clink Prison Museum
Fashion and Textile Museum
Golden Hinde
Sky Garden
Tate Modern
Tower Bridge
Tower of London
White Cube (Art gallery)

London

The Chocolate Show London

As a chocolate lover, going to The Chocolate Show London was a must go do event. Who doesn't love chocolate? I want to meet them. I paid 15 GBP at the door, since I didn't book in advance for a bit less, for this guilty pleasure. Minutes later, I found myself overdosing on complimentary chocolate samples. Some booths and vendors were more chocolatey than others. How exciting is it to read literature on chocolate with no samples? Boring! At least give out a voucher for future use, right?

The chocolate runway show was very entertaining. One vendor made amazing chocolate heels/stilettos that could have given Jimmy Choo or Manolo Blahnik, a real walk for their money. The Sex & the City gals might be able to wear shoes like that, but they are totally impractical for a travel writer who needs to wear sneakers and ballet flats. Those heels were almost as cool as Dorothy's sparkly ruby red sequin slippers from the Wizard of Oz movie. I saw them years ago for free at the Smithsonian National Museum of American History in Washington, DC.

(October 2016)

ITALY & USA

Eating Pizza in Naples & Chicago

You'll dine on Neapolitan pizza or Margherita pizza
(tomatoes, basil, EVOO, and mozzarella cheese)
when you're in Naples, Italy.

Naples, Italy Pizzerias:

L'antica Pizzeria da Michele (damichele.net)

Pizzeria Brandi

Pizzeria Di Matteo (pizzeriadimatteo.com)

Pizzeria Gino Sorbillo (sorbillo.it)

When you're in the Windy City of Chicago, IL (USA)
it's all about deep-dish pizza, thanks to Uno's chubby
creation.

Chicago, IL Pizzerias:

Giordano's (Stuffed pizza)

Lou Malnati's

Pequod's Pizza

Uno Pizzeria & Grill (unos.com)

I sure hope you enjoy your slice wherever and
however, whether you hold it, fold it, or cut it!

Buon appetito! Enjoy!

DENMARK, SWEDEN, UK & USA

Hygge, Fika, Tea & Coffee Breaks

A short afternoon break is a universal ritual, but different countries have different names for it. The Danes have a cozy hygge and the Swedish enjoy a fika. It's common to pair a hot drink with a sweet dessert such as a sugary & spicy cinnamon roll.

The English drink coffee, of course, but they really love their cuppa tea. In fact, many of them even bring their own teabags on vacation. They enjoy afternoon tea, champagne afternoon tea & cream tea.

In the good old USA, they take a daily coffee break with a hot drink from somewhere like Starbucks®, Dunkin'®, an urban jungle coffee truck, or an on-site company break room/lounge. Some might even pair it with something sweet from the baked goods case or a sweet or salty snack from a vending machine that works, hopefully. Hipsters can be found somewhere cool, wearing something cool, and working at a cool job at a cool company where they can coolly sip one for free. Or from Intelligentsia or another cool coffee/tea joint that serves pricey, organic, sustainable, ethical, or all the above hot drinks.

UK & USA

Curry: East London & NYC's East Village

Although the Hindoostane Coffee House in London's Marylebone neighborhood (City of Westminster), is no longer there, London is full of curry houses. There are more than 8,000 Indian and Bangladeshi restaurants in the UK. If you ever make it to Birmingham and are craving Indian food, the Balti Triangle awaits. Or you can venture over to Bradford which has won The British Curry Awards (britishcurryaward.co.uk) a few times. Or perhaps go for a curry somewhere on Manchester's Curry Mile?

Curry competes with fish & chips as a top take away meal in the UK. If you've never tried curry sauce on chips, try it. It tastes amazing! Brick Lane in East London which is filled with hipsters and bankers is the best place to chow down on a curry since there's tons of curry houses to choose from. Check out the cool street art before sunset in the nearby arty neighborhood, Shoreditch. If you're craving or curious about any Indian sweets, stop by Rajmahal Sweets at 57 Brick Lane. For Indian grocery shopping, go to Taj Store at 112 Brick Lane.

London's mini chain, Dishoom, will have you feeling like you stepped out of the Big Smoke and into an old Irani café in Bombay, especially after you've tasted its food & drink.

If you're in NYC, you can be transported to India in the Big Apple if you walk around 26th Street to 30th Street on Lexington Avenue. As an ex-New Yorker of 17 years, I lived in nearby Gramercy Park, so felt like I was kind of in India most of the time except for the absence of cows in the streets. Both NYC and India have crowds and chaos. It's hard to forget a small Indian spice shop there that was chock full of exotic, fragrant, and colorful spices & candies, etc. It reminded me of the book, "The Mistress of Spices." A great place to get a take-out or a no-frills simple cafeteria like meal there is from Curry in a Hurry at 119 Lexington Avenue. Many NYC yellow cab taxi drivers get their food fuel here before refueling their cab or starting/ending their shift.

You can walk to NYC's East Village (EV) or Little India on East 6th Street (1st & 2nd Avenues) where many Bollywood-like decorative restaurants can be found.

Eater Beware: The curries that you might eat at a curry house in London, NYC, or wherever might taste a little bit different from the ones you eat in India. Same but different. And the culture and atmosphere in which one eats them whether surrounded by locals or in a venue where you might be the only woman not wearing a sari or a man not wearing a kurta and dhoti can only add flavor to the dining experience.

UK, USA & ITALY

Shrimp Scampi

When you order shrimp scampi in the UK, you'll receive fried breaded shrimp & chips (French Fries). It's what the Americans call shrimp in the basket.

If you order shrimp scampi in the USA and Italy, you'll be served some type of pasta such as linguine, angel hair, fettucine, spaghetti, or rice with shrimp in a garlic, olive oil, and white wine sauce.

Eating a Meal

In the USA, dinner usually includes an appetizer, main course or entrée, and dessert.

The British menu consists of a starter, main course, and pudding or afters (dessert).

The Italians might order antipasti, a first course or il primo such as pasta, a second course or il secondo such as fish or meat, and a side dish (contorno). Dolce (dessert) follows with a sweet such as gelato or tiramisu. Locals tend to eat a bigger meal for lunch.

USA

CA

Southern CA

California Avocado Festival

Lady luck was on my side when I stumbled upon the three-day annual California Avocado Festival (**avofest.com**) in Carpinteria. I'd been working in Santa Barbara when I heard about it and nothing was going to stop me from going to this superfood event. Nothing! Nada! I'd be green with envy if I didn't go.

The fairground was your typical one except avocados were the main attraction here. Admission was free and live music was featured, too. The local cheer leading squad made and sold homemade lumpy bumpy green guacamole from a huge vat. I was tempted to jump in to get my fill. Wouldn't that be fun? You might look like the Hulk or a Green Goddess after, but who cares?

I indulged in an avocado brownie with a chocolate exterior and avocado interior and then licked away at a scoop of avocado ice cream which hit the spot on a hot & sunny CA day.

Travel Tip: Carpinteria is about a 15-minute drive from Santa Barbara or about a 1-3/4 hour drive from LA only if there's no traffic.   *(October 2015)*

San Francisco
Chocolate, Fish & Sourdough Bread

Food has an origin or birthplace just like people do. When you arrive in a city, suburb, or rural area you might see signs for factory tours, outlets, or you might just smell whatever item that the area is famous for.

When you arrive in the Bay City of San Francisco, you'll smell the faint scent of sourdough bread in the air, thanks to The Boudin Bakery. It's been baking sourdough bread for more than 170 years, way before it became a foodie trend and food staple. Apparently, San Fran's foggy and cool climate might have something to do with it. Location!! It's a similar gastro-geo concept to the nearby vineyards of Napa & Sonoma which are well suited for wine production.

As you approach Fisherman's Wharf, the air in this tech city smells a bit fishy and salty and then turns chocolatey as you near Ghirardelli Square. And then it's on to North Beach, with its garlicky Italian scent, and over to Chinatown and Japantown for a whiff of Far East fragrant foodie scents!

Santa Barbara
The Urban Wine Trail & The Funk Zone

If you like wine and Southern California, you should see the movie, "Sideways," or better yet take a trip to the red-roofed coastal city of Santa Barbara. You'll feel like you landed in some kind of wonderful urban wine vineyard. It's a much different feel than arriving at a rustic looking vineyard in Napa, France, or Italy. Different is good! It's all good!

I really didn't know what to expect from a trip to the artsy and gastronomic Funk Zone & the Urban Wine Trail (urbanwinetrailsb.com). Should I have great, I mean grape expectations? What I found were more than 20 wineries in town with tastings and tours just waiting to be strolled to. When you're done looking at, swirling, sniffing, sipping, and savoring all kinds of wines, it might be a good idea to call an Uber or get a Lyft, so you're not walking sideways, dontcha think? I think so!

Travel Tips:
santabarbaraca.com
visitcalifornia.com

FL

Key West

Kermit's Key West Key Lime Shoppe

Kermit's for all things key lime! Think barbecue sauce, cake, candy, cookies, fudge, honey, hot sauce, jelly, olive oil, peanuts, pies, and spices, etcetera.

Edible souvenirs are best! I'm sure your family, friends, and co-workers will enjoy them more than a mug or keychain. Check out **keylimeshop.com**.

Key West

Bars, Clothing Optional & Hemingway

Once you reach Duval Street, you'll be spoiled with a choice of bars such as The Bull & Whistle. You might even be tempted to go au naturel at the Garden of Eden. Sloppy Joe's which is in a different spot now and Captain Tony's Saloon had Hemingway as a customer. Ignore any bars that opened after 1962 claiming to have Ernest as a customer as it's just not true.

Rum in Key West: Key West First Legal Rum Distillery.
Sunset & Drinks Tip: Mallory Square. Watch the daily sun dip and fade away around 5 PM.

GA

Atlanta
World of Coca-Cola

After not drinking soda for about 25 years other than a few sips of a new flavor once in a blue moon, I found myself in the World of Coca-Cola. My curiosity for all things new and different coupled with my Marketing background and drink FOMO, was not going to let me leave the peach state without going to this interactive soda museum (**worldofcoca-cola.com**).

The best part is Taste It! where you can try world flavors. I didn't try all 100 flavors as I felt myself going into a bit of a sugar shock after sipping around a dozen sodas, but I still had a lot of fun even for a non-soda drinker! I was transported to Italy via The Beverly, a before dinner drink (apéritif). Then it was on to India via Thums Up, a spicy soda, and down to Thailand via a Fanta Melon Frosty, a sweet melon soda.

Other cool stuff to see here is Coca-Cola bottle art, artifacts, and the bottling line. Unfortunately, the secret formula was safely locked up in the vault!

LA

New Orleans

Weather Resistant Cajun & Creole Cuisine

It's been almost 30 years since I was in New Orleans, which is hard to believe, since the food there is so diverse and delicious! And I live to eat and eat to live!

Although Hurricane Katrina came and went, "The Big Easy," continues to serve up food from years old family recipes and honor traditions. Certain dishes might come and go on the food scene, but I'm happy to hear from family and friends who've recently visited, that they enjoyed their chicory coffee from Café Du Monde and French Market. They didn't seem to worry about their waistline as they told me they ate one powdery and sugary beignet after another. And they couldn't eat enough crawfish, Gulf oysters, gumbo, jambalaya, and Po' Boys!

If you visit during Mardi Gras, be prepared for a crazy, crowded, and loud time.   *(Mardi Gras 1994)*

neworleans.com

MA

Vineyard Haven (Martha's Vineyard)
How Can a Vineyard Be Dry?

How can a vineyard be dry? My thoughts, exactly!

I'd been to the island of Martha's Vineyard before, but I didn't know Vineyard Haven was a dry town until I worked there one summer. How dry was I? Dry. Very dry. This meant taking a ride over to Oak Bluffs to enjoy a drink which was fine as the town is pretty like a picture with its many colorful gingerbread like houses. Or it was over to Edgartown with its preppy like Nantucket feel. *(Summer 2003)*

Travel Tips: Vineyard Haven (Tisbury) might be a wet town now, so if you're headed that way and want to wet your whistle, it would be best to check before going.

Getting a car reservation for July & August when the water is the warmest on the Cape & The Islands can be hard if you don't reserve way in advance. Crocker Inn is located near the ferry dock in Vineyard Haven and its innkeepers, Jeff & Jynell, are lovely.

capecodchamber.org

MD

Whitehaven

The Red Roost Crabhouse & Restaurant

On the way back from a family wedding, some family members and I took a teeny tiny ferry across the Wicomico River to the Whitehaven Hotel B & B (whitehavenhotel.com) on Maryland's Eastern Shore. The friendly boat captain entertained my nephew, Nicholas, as we made the short scenic crossing on the Whitehaven Ferry. The ride made me remember other ferry crossings which carried myself and other excited holidaymakers from places such as Woods Hole, MA (Cape Cod) to the island of Martha's Vineyard and from Dover, England to Calais, France. However, those were on larger ferries which charged a pretty penny for transporting cars, while this ferry was free and could only carry a few cars and up to 6 passengers.

The charming innkeeper who resembled the actress, Diane Lane, checked us in and suggested we go to the Red Roost (**theredroost.com**) in nearby Quantico when we inquired about a restaurant. As soon as she roomed us, we flew the coop and headed on over to the roost.

Upon entering this rustic dining establishment, we felt like we'd died and gone to seafood heaven. MD is well known for crabs and Old Bay seasoning. This herb & spice seasoning that comes in a yellow, blue, red & white metal can makes a great souvenir gift, too.

During dinner, we saw crabs in various forms pass by our table: Crabs, Crab Cakes, Crab Dip, Crab Pots, Lump Crab, Snow Crab Legs, Steamed Blue Crabs, Crab Soup, and Roasted Corn & Crab Chowder. If crab isn't your thing, you can always stuff your face full of Clams, Oysters, Seafood Platters, Sea Scallops, and Old Bay Spiced Steamed Shrimp.

Omnivores can feast on steaks and ribs and there are salads for vegetarians to nibble on. Truth be told, the fried chicken was amazing! It could easily win a blue ribbon at a country fair! A real find in MD with a fun atmosphere!

(May 2012)

MI
Detroit
Mexicantown

Mexico in Detroit? You betcha!!

When you can't travel to Mexico whether you're time or cash poor, but can get to Detroit, head on over to Bagley Avenue and Vernor Hwy, for tortillas, guacamole, and margaritas.

Mexican Food on Bagley Avenue (Around 2600-3460) & Bagley Street:

Algo Especial Super Market, Evie's Tamales, La Gloria Bakery, Los Galanes, Mexican Town Restaurant, Mexican Village, Taqueria Lupita, and Xochimilco.

Mexican Food on (Around 2669-4336) Vernor Hwy:

Armando's Mexican Restaurant, Ice Cream La Michoacana, MexicanTown Bakery, Tamaleria Nuevo Leon, and Taqueria La Mexicana.

Travel Tip: Stop by the Detroit Mexicantown Int. Welcome Center at 2835 Bagley Avenue. **visitdetroit.com**

NJ
Atlantic City
Salt Water Taffy

"Skinny long Fralinger's or chubby little James'?" There's nothing like a beach sweet such as salt water taffy, fudge, or cotton candy.

Food is memory! Whether salty or sweet, food has the power to create everlasting memories. Hopefully, happy, crazy, or laugh out loud really funny memories!

The memories of the anticipation and excitement of seeing our grandparents and their gifting us with sweet beach treats comforted us when it was no longer possible to see them.

Food is best enjoyed when it's shared. Although, there were many tense moments and first dibs calls when it came time to choose a flavor as the taffy box was passed around. Hmm? Should I take Banana, Cherry, Chocolate, Coconut, Lemon, Licorice, Molasses, Orange, Peach, Peppermint, Spearmint, Teaberry or Vanilla? Yum! How many steps do I need to take on the Atlantic City boardwalk to burn up all these calories? 10,000? 10,000,000? Do you think Miss America eats any salt water taffy?

atlanticcitynj.com

NY

NYC

Bird's Nest Soup & Shark Fin Soup

My Burmese boyfriend looked forward to this day for days, weeks, and months. He might have even been as excited as the bride-to-be and groom-to-be, but for very different reasons. He thought of nothing else and talked about nothing else other than bird's nest soup and shark fin soup. I, on the other hand, didn't think of them at all. I was only curious about what my fortune cookie message might be.

I was just happy that he was so happy. Over the next few weeks while he was dreaming of soup, I was dreaming about sleep since I always felt tired from working at a tech startup.

When the big day finally arrived, we headed to the venue that was located off Canal Street in NYC's vast and chaotic Chinatown. Upon our arrival, we were directed to an upper floor of a huge banquet room that could easily accommodate 200-300 guests. The room was decorated with many gold decorative accents and gold blingy mirrors. It was chock full of many red and gold festive symbols and ornaments, too. Red symbolizes happiness, luck, and fertility. Hopefully, this union would result in a "double happy" marriage and not end in divorce. Gold symbolizes wealth.

Chinese Wedding Attendance Tip: Never wear red to a Chinese wedding as the bride will change a few times and will wear a red dress at some point. You wouldn't want to upstage her. Do not wear a white or black dress as they are worn at Chinese funerals. A pastel dress would be fine to wear.

When the big moment came to order either bird's nest soup or shark fin soup, I politely asked the waiter if they had any wonton soup. Wrong move! Seven pairs of eyes wide open in shock just looked at me. Could my cheeks turn any redder? You would've thought I had dropped my chopsticks and bad luck was waiting for me around the corner. I just really like wonton soup, but quickly ordered the shark fin soup.

I enthusiastically oohed and aahed after a few sips. I then graciously offered some to my beau who had ordered the bird's nest soup. I triumphantly smiled as he accepted the bowl from me and sipped and slurped away while I breathed a sigh of relief. Now, that's what I call a good girlfriend! And then it was on to the next seven mystery courses.

(Circa late 1990's)

Food Shopping in NYC's Chinatown

The procurement of food is just as important as cooking and eating it both near and far. Gastronomic experiences and encounters can be downright weird, wonderful, interesting, cultural, over the top, fancy-schmancy, and Michelin starred. And just plain scary if insects and brains are involved!

Eating what you know is a sensible and safe bet. However, not eating what you don't know, eliminates bragging rights or culinary travel tales that you can regale family & friends with forever.

Sometimes you've just got to suck it up (carpe diem) and do the adventurous or polite thing. Hopefully, it will result in fun memories and no nightmares.

In the early 90's, my boyfriend and I helped his mother with her Saturday afternoon food shopping a few times. After picking her up from her Tai Chi exercise class that she took with other elders in Columbus Park, we would head to NYC's Chinatown.

A trip to NYC's Chinatown is a good way for New Yorkers and others to experience Asia. They can eat all kinds of Chinese food, save money, save time, and avoid jetlag. Foreign tongues, crowds, and chaos are present here, too. The only way you'll know you're not in Asia is as soon as you leave Chinatown, you'll be thrust into garlicky Little Italy & stylish SoHo.

Much time and care were spent in procuring ingredients for the coming week's meals for extended family and friends. I liked watching Mrs. Lee as she wandered from one store or stall to another from Canal Street to Mott Street and over to East Broadway. She acknowledged and greeted familiar vendors and was curious yet hesitant with new ones. She carefully sourced exotic looking fruits & veggies from baskets and cartons, whole fishes with their eyes intact from fish tanks or beds of ice, and wiggly looking seafood from plastic buckets. Almost all the names and descriptions were written in standard Chinese but thanks to the universality of numbers, I understood their prices. This was a big help when I compared prices with other stalls, shops, and street vendors along the way.

Sometimes before we left Manhattan for Queens, we would treat ourselves to a bubble tea with a thick straw, which allowed tapioca pearls to effortlessly glide up them. That was then and this is now, so I would probably bring my own bamboo or stainless steel straw for eco & green reasons. You really need a thick straw to enjoy those chubby tapioca balls.

Upon arriving in Queens, Mrs. Lee would get down to business peeling, cutting, frying, steaming, and sautéing all sorts of veggies, chicken, pork, and fish. The rice cooker seemed to be going the whole day, so that was one less dish to prepare, which left more time for making dumplings from scratch. When dinner was ready, I would sit down under one roof with a large family that spanned three generations. The more the merrier! I got used to everyone yelling at each other as I realized they weren't mad at each other. It was just how they communicated.

After witnessing all the efforts, expense, and love that this kind woman put into cooking food for her family and me, there was no way I couldn't eat any of this Burmese banquet. The act of sharing food is love and kindness in action. She cooked with ancient Chinese secrets, centuries old family recipes, pride and love for her country, and a whole lot of love. I owed her my full attention, appreciation, and respect. I would have to have each dish explained to me before I slowly dug in, but the important thing is that I dug in and broadened my knowledge of Asian cuisine.

Years later, I impressed locals when I told them to enjoy their Mohinga, Burmese Rice & Fish Curry, Lahpet Thoke and Gyin Thoke, etc. Thanks, Mrs. Lee!

(Circa early 1990's)

NYC

Chocolate Bars at Dylan's Candy Bar

If Willy Wonka were alive today, he'd have some stiff competition in Dylan Lauren of Dylan's Candy Bar **(dylanscandybar.com)**. For about $3.25 (Prices as of February 2021), chocoholics can indulge in any of these cool flavored candy bars: Bacon, Birthday Cake, Brownie Batter, NY Milk Chocolate Pretzel, Popping Candy, Potato Chip, Red Velvet, and S'mores, etcetera. There's even a Junk Food Aisle Chocolate Bar Bundle! These flavors are definitely more fun and creative than your average chocolate bar flavors. However, I'm not one to turn down any boring flavors such as Cookies & Cream or Milk Chocolate!

"Thank you, thank you, Dylan, for making candy instead of clothes." I wonder if her father, Ralph, likes chocolate and candy?

NYC (City Island)
New England Seafood in the Bronx?

Stepping foot on this tiny little island in the Bronx (**cityisland.com**) is like arriving in the Hamptons or Cape Cod & the Islands (Martha's Vineyard and Nantucket) without having to deal with all the traffic nightmares of I-495, I-95, I-84, or NY-27 E.

On a beautiful Indian summer afternoon, I made the trek from NYC via the #6 subway followed by a 10-minute ride on bus# 29, to enjoy a bit and bites of New England in New York. This tiny town in the Long Island Sound has many seafood shops along with a boating community, cute houses, and quaint churches.

If you love fish and all kinds of seafood, Sammy's (**sammysfishbox.com & sammysshrimpbox.com**) located on City Island Avenue, won't disappoint. You'll sea, I mean see, a lot of fish from the sea on Sammy's vast seafood menu such as blue fish, calamari, clams, clam strips, crab cakes, crab legs, fillet of sole, fish & chips, lobster, mussels, oysters, salmon, scallops, shrimp, swordfish, and tilapia. You can have some items baked, broiled, fried, raw, or stuffed. And there's steak for omnivores. Just remember to leave room for dessert! Enjoy!   *(September 2017)*

NYC & The Hamptons
Food: Sex, Orgasms & The Affair

Cupcakes (Sex & The City):

The popular TV show, Sex & the City, made the Magnolia Bakery at 401 Bleecker Street in NYC's West Village, a cupcake haunt. Pastel colored frosted cupcakes as well as classic flavors like vanilla and chocolate sweetly seduce sweet tooths at this "home sweet home" like shop. You can buy pies, cakes, cookies, and cheesecakes here, too. If there's a line, perhaps head on over to Billy's Bakery or Sprinkles.

Pastrami on Rye (Faking It) in NYC:

If you want to have what Sally's having like in the hit movie, "When Harry Met Sally," go to **Katz's Deli** in NYC's Lower East Side, which is close to SoHo. I can guarantee you that you'll get a tasty pastrami on rye, but I can't guarantee you'll have the Big O. 2nd Ave Deli is a popular deli, too.

Lobster Rolls (The Affair) in The Hamptons

If the Solloways had eaten lunch at Rowdy Hall, The Blue Parrot, La Fondita, or taken out a tub of crispy Southern Fried Chicken from Brent's General Store then Alison and Noah wouldn't have met. And then there wouldn't have been an affair. Or a TV show about The Affair. Life without good TV to watch would be pretty boring!

Alison and Noah met at The Lobster Roll aka LUNCH (**lobsterroll.com**) in Amagansett near East Hampton. It's a logical seafood dining choice for locals, day-trippers, holidaymakers, quarter-share, half-share & full-share summer house renters, weekenders, the rich & famous, summer people, celebrities, and Manhattanites.

Fortunately, they didn't stop to eat at The Golden Pear Café in Southampton, Bridgehampton Candy Kitchen, or Sam's Restaurant, and Cittanuova in East Hampton. Although, they're all delicious!

Helen, Noah's wife, always seemed like such a stalwart person and the reliable glue that held the Solloway family together even though her life fell apart while Noah's ascended and descended.

OR

Portland

Salt & Straw's Crazy Ice Cream Flavors

I arrived in Portland from Seattle on a Greyhound bus one summer evening two hours later than planned due to delays. This meant that I'd have two hours less to pursue my Portland foodie goals! Oh well! Better late than never! Nothing was going to stop this foodie from going to Salt & Straw at 838 NW 23rd Avenue (**saltandstraw.com**) and I mean nothing!! The things we do for the love of ice cream and bragging rights!

The quest for wacky artisanal ice cream flavors involved getting into a very long line or queue as the English say. Call me crazy! Not all was lost, though, as I picked up some secret local foodie tips during the wait.

Finally, my turn to order came and did I ever order! A scoop of Pear & Blue Cheese ice cream and a scoop of Olive Oil ice cream. Success!! I think I would've lost it if they ran out of those flavors after all the hoops I jumped through to procure them. I would have been mad as heck! Of course, there were other wacky and unique flavors, but my heart was set on what it was set on.

My taste buds didn't know what to think after a few licks of these crazy gourmet flavors. OMG!! Definitely different!! I licked away and then raced to the airport to make my red-eye flight to Chicago. How I wished there'd been a scoop shop or kiosk at the Portland International Airport. It would be an ideal location for "arriving and departing" ice cream connoisseurs and to build brand awareness.

The next time I enjoyed a scoop from Salt & Straw was at their branch in Studio City, CA. And there was no line! I was able to leisurely lick away at my tasty scoop of honey lavender ice cream while I chit-chatted with my girlfriend, Lisa. And then I found myself racing off to LA's Union Station to catch my bus. It's funny, but it seems like I'm always catching some form of public transportation somewhere to see, do, or eat something or other! Go figure!

(August 2016)

(TravelPortland.com)

PA

Lancaster

Amish Food

The best way to describe Amish food or PA Dutch food is as very basic home cooked and cozy food. It's much tastier than plane food.

The ideal place to sample it is at Dienner's Country Restaurant (dienners.com) in Ronks, PA, which is about 20 minutes from Lancaster. Years ago, I had roast chicken there, which was hearty, filling, comforting, and served in a no-frills atmosphere. I'm not sure if there have ever been Michelin stars awarded for plain and non-fussy Amish cuisine, but you never know! Dienner's offers all sorts of buffets for breakfast, lunch, and dinner. It closes early around 6 PM-7 PM and is not open on Sunday. Don't leave without ordering a slice of shoofly pie.

If you can't make it to Amish Country, but if you come across a Boston Market or a Marie Callender's Restaurant & Bakery (USA restaurant chains) on your travels, stop and order the rotisserie chicken or chicken pot pie and some side dishes. You'll get the idea after a few mouthfuls. I can't promise that you'll bump into any Amish or Mennonites but who knows?

Philadelphia
A "Taste of Summer" Mural

As I passed the "Taste of Summer" mural at 1312 Spruce Street in Center City Philly, my mind was flooded with "good times" memories. This colorful artwork reminded me of a trip to Tuscany where the preparation and sharing of food & wine with friends was the highlight of the day. The type of pasta, sauce, pizza, and insalata we should make was a daily question. Of course, cooking anything was only possible after we'd sourced our ingredients from markets and supermarkets before they closed for the afternoon riposo (the siesta). Otherwise, we'd be having a famine instead of an Italian feast!

The seven of us laughed, talked, debated about everything under the sun, and played cards & board games surrounded by cypress trees and red poppies while the Mediterranean sun kept us warm. These long al fresco lunches lasted anywhere from 1-3 hours. Food creates memories! Good times! What else do you need in life? Oh, I forgot, a job to pay for it all! *(2001-Siena, Italy & September 2017-Philadelphia, PA)*

Visit **muralarts.org** to check out other Philly murals. **Philly Italian Foodie Tip:** Go to the Italian Market on South 9th Street to procure all your ingredients.

Philadelphia

World Flavors at Reading Terminal Mkt

If you're a real foodie and find yourself in Center City Philly, you can eat the world at Reading Terminal Market **(ReadingTerminalMarket.org)** at 12th & Arch Streets. Just think of all the fun and delicious food selfies you can take here!

This vast indoor food market that's housed in a historic building has almost 100 stalls and has been pleasing and feeding foodies and fuss budgets for 120+ years. Food from every corner of the world, as well as field to fork, farm to table, and hook to table food can all be found here. And enjoyed in a casual communal eating area or taken to go. On site, is the honky-tonk like Down Home Diner which serves comfort food in booths or at the counter. It's a great place to eat breakfast, lunch, or an early dinner.

The food hall is located close to the Greyhound bus station and the convention center, so it's ideal for foodie and worldly tourists and conference goers who want variety. For locals, it's a great place to go food shopping.

Enjoy!!

Philadelphia

Philly Cheesesteaks

The Philadelphia Cheesesteak is a hot foodie topic. The mere mention of this hot, juicy, gooey, and cheesy creation can be a conversation starter or one that can quickly turn into a heated debate as locals all have their favorite joint. I wonder where Rocky Balboa went for a cheesesteak? Do you think he ate more than one when he was getting ready for a boxing match?

Tourists and locals seek out these cheesesteak joints:
Campo's (camposdeli.com)
Jim's (jimssouthstreet.com)
Geno's (genosteaks.com)
Govinda's (govindasphilly.com)
Pat's King of Steaks (patskingofsteaks.com)

There is even a Philly Cheesesteak Tour.

I was once stopped by a tourist who wanted to bring the famous sandwich to her husband in NYC as a Philly souvenir. Fried chicken is ok hot or cold, but a juicy cheesesteak oozing with cheese, onions, and whatever other toppings must always be eaten ASAP right on the spot. Any hot food item that's ordered and not quickly gobbled up while still hot is just plain wrong. There's no such thing as a cold cheesesteak. Or ice cream soup. No such thing! I explained to her that this wouldn't be a good gift. In fact, it would be a terrible gift as it would make any Philly cheesesteak taste less than it was. There's no way this hot & cheesy creation from any sandwich shop could make a two-hour trip and retain its spectacular flavor. The taste would be compromised even if she took Amtrak's Acela Express back to the Big Apple and Amtrak's Northeast Regional train, Septa & NJ Transit trains, and Megabus were not options.

I suggested that she treat her husband for a weekend in Philly, City of Brotherly Love, where they could eat at all the city's great restaurants & bars, devour freshly made hot cheesesteaks, see the Liberty Bell, the LOVE sculpture, and great Impressionist art at The Barnes Foundation.

In the meantime, she should just get a pretzel from Philly Pretzel Factory or a donut or some fried chicken from Federal Donuts. After all, it's the thought that counts, right?

Philly Tips: Philadelphia Magazine's Best of Philly issue is full of the best food & drink venues.

discoverphl.com
visitphilly.com

SC
Charleston
Lowcountry Cuisine

You'll work up an appetite after touring all those Southern plantations & gardens such as Boone Hall, Magnolia Plantation, and Middleton Place. Or from frolicking on some of South Carolina's lovely beaches such as Folly Beach or Isle of Palms, and when you do, you'll be spoiled for choice.

Be prepared to see these Lowcountry foods on menus all over town: Boiled Peanuts, Collard Greens, Cornbread, Fried Chicken, Fried Green Tomatoes, Oysters, and Shrimp & Grits. Wash it all down with a Sweet Tea.

Don't forget to stop by the Charleston City Market where you can see sweetgrass baskets being made, buy some spices, and chow down on some flaky biscuits.

If you never make it down South, you can kind of sort of get a taste of Southern & New Orleans food at Bubba Gump Shrimp Co. restaurant chain.
charlestongateway.com
charlestoncvb.com

WASHINGTON, D.C

Eating Native Cuisine

Hmm? What the heck do American Indians eat? After a stop at the Mitsitam Native Foods Café at the National Museum of the American Indian (NMAI) (americanindian.si.edu) in DC, I had the answers to my question.

The café is appropriately named Mitsitam which means, "Let's eat," in both the Piscataway and Delaware languages. Eating native means, you'll find yourself chowing down on foods such as Bison Burgers, Bison Steak, Buffalo Chili, Corn Totopos, Fry Bread, and Lomo Saltado, etcetera.

The museum's wavy and curvy Kasota limestone exterior is way cool, too! It's no tepee! The green grounds have bronze and clay sculptures and running water features that are so lovely and refreshing in this capital city. And the best thing about this place, is that it's free, for all of us to see!   *(August 2017)*

Washington, DC Travel Tip: This city is chock full of "free to see" diverse, artistic, beautiful, educational, historical, inspiring, interesting, and scientific museums!!

washington.org

LAST BUT NOT LEAST

Food: Colors, Scents, Sounds & Textures

Colors:

The color of a food makes an everlasting impression or memory whether it's one color such as a yellowy yellow lemon from Italy, an orangey orange from Croatia or Florida, or white fluffy Greek yogurt. Or it can be multi-colored such as an orange yellow gold curry powder from India.

Two of the most colorful foods I've seen, eaten, and enjoyed so far are the Rainbow Cake at the Hummingbird Bakery in London. This colorful cake consists of 6 colored layers (red, orange, yellow, green, blue, and violet purple). Yes, rainbows really do appear after a London shower! And the tie-dye bagel in Philadelphia, PA at Chestnut Street Philly Bagels (chestnutbagels.com)!

Scents:

You could be wearing a blindfold, yet the smell of a scent wafting out of a kitchen or a restaurant, would give the cuisine away such as a garlicky Italian pasta or pizza, a fragrant coconut or spicy Indian curry, a freshly baked French baguette, or Southern fried chicken. The nose always knows.

Sounds:

Whether you're dining out in Mexico or at a local Mexican restaurant, the sizzling sound of a hot fajita as it's making its way to your table, is how our food can speak to us. "I'm hot, so proceed with caution."

The sound of a fellow moviegoer making loud popcorn crunching noises is probably one we can all do without, that is, unless we're the one making the annoying crunching sounds.

Textures:

A food's texture can be experienced by touching it with your tongue, hand, or both.

Touching a tortilla chip via your hand & tongue can feel like you're about to eat a piece of corny sandpaper. Hopefully, one that's loaded with creamy lumpy bumpy green guacamole. Noodles or pasta are usually silky slippery squiggly or chewy and glide down one's throat easily. Cereals and crackers tend to have a rough crumbly and grainy texture. Nothing can feel smoother on one's tongue than applesauce or creamy ice cream. And let's not even get into sticky honey leaving us with sticky fingers!

Foodie Trends

Food has the power to be short-lived like a trend or to stick around for a while like the avocado has done in the form of smashed avocado on toast. Although, the avocado has been a staple in CA cuisine and Japanese sushi rolls for many years. For more, on avocados in Australia, please refer to the story in this book, "The Avocado Farmer in Queensland."

Eggs Restaurants

The saying, "not to put all your eggs in one basket," is a good one. And fortunately, you don't have to, since all types of eggs-cellent eggs can be ordered at any of the following egg outposts: Eggslut **(eggslut.com)** in USA, UK, and Asia or Yolk®. **(eatyolk.com)** chain in the USA. Although, scrambled, soft-boiled or hard-boiled eggs can be enjoyed in any old diner or in your very own kitchen.

Cereal Restaurants

Going out for a bowl of cereal was a trend for a while in DTLA CA & London but the recent global health crisis might have forced some businesses to rethink their business models. Fortunately, the Cereal Killer Café **(cerealkillercafe.co.uk)** in London sells all kinds of sweet & sugary cereals online. It's a very fun way to start your day, especially if you're WFH.

Poke Restaurants

The best way to describe poke is that it's almost, but not quite the Hawaiian version of Japanese chirashi. A chirashi bowl usually has a few types of fish & vinegary sushi rice. A poke bowl usually has tuna or another fish with rice or no rice. Both have veggies but different seasonings. They're kind of sort of like the same dish but kind of sort of different.

Cronuts® & Cruffins

When two similar foods mate, a new food craze sweeps the world. A croissant & a doughnut got busy and the Cronut® was born with a bit of help from the French pastry chef, Dominique Ansel, of Dominique Ansel Bakery in NYC. If you want to eat a cruffin, which is the marriage of a muffin & a croissant, go to Lune Croissanterie in Melbourne, Australia or to Mr. Holmes Bakehouse in San Fran.

After these pastries were born, it seemed like bakeries all over were mating pastries to invent crazy new sugary and doughy ones with funky sounding names. I can't imagine what a threesome between a doughnut, a muffin & a croissant, or a foursome (Is that even possible?) between a doughnut, a muffin, a croissant & an éclair would yield!!

dominiqueanselny.com & lunecroissanterie.com

Strange Foods All Over the World

FYI: Proceed with caution!

Australia: Crocodile, Kangaroo, and Emu.

After a spontaneous and scenic plane ride of the Daintree Rainforest on a teeny tiny plane with laid-back "no worries" Derry, it was time to eat at the nearby outdoor café that served Australian fare.

Our newly acquired bravery and curiosity found us capriciously ordering some crocodile carpaccio. The thin raw slices of reptile tasted like reptile. *(September 2001)*

Australia Lodging Tips: PK's Jungle Village in Cape Tribulation is ideal for backpackers. For tree house style eco-friendly accommodations, check out Cockatoo Hill Retreat (cockatoohillretreat.com.au).

England: Bangers and Mash, Bubble & Squeak, Crumble, Eton Mess, Knickerbocker Glory, Ploughman's Lunch, Scotch Eggs, Spotted Dick, Toad in the Hole, Yorkshire Puddings, and Welsh Rarebit.

The first time I ate Eton Mess; I thought it should be called, "I'm eating a mess." This tasty strawberries, meringue, and whipped cream dessert looks so pretty, but just have some napkins handy to clean up the mess after you've indulged in eating one. The same goes for Knickerbocker Glory which is another lovely big mess of a messy but awesome dessert!

Starchy Yorkshire Puddings have nothing to do with pudding or dessert and have everything to do with a Sunday roast.

Spotted Dick has nothing to do with what your dirty mind might be thinking. It has everything to do with afters or pudding which is what the British call dessert. Don't even get me started on Toad in the hole.

France: Frogs' Legs.

You'd be surprised but frogs' legs taste a bit like chicken, so if you can eat one than why not the other? The best ones I ever ate were made by a Frenchie at Le Grenier in Vineyard Haven on Martha's Vineyard, MA in the summer of 2003. They were cooked in white wine and garlic and were so succulent and moist. While the restaurant isn't there anymore, memories of those frogs' legs are. Speaking of frogs, I've eaten some of the best French food outside of France, but it has always been cooked by a Frenchie such as the Cronut® from Dominique Ansel. They sure know their way around the kitchen!

Iceland: Sour Ram's Testicles, Fermented Shark, Pungent Shark, Whale Meat, Boiled Sheep's Heads, and Puffin.

I heard talk about how fermented shark might help with some illnesses when I was in Reykjavík, but who knows if that's true? A few Icelanders told me it tasted a bit like ammonia. Yuck! Not for me, no thank you! Do not eat any without consulting your doctor! Fish tends to be pickled and preserved in the land of fire & ice. It's a big part of the Icelandic diet besides black licorice and chocolate bars with licorice bits.

I learned there are more puffins than Icelanders in Iceland. That got me thinking and maybe even caused me to worry. Can puffins eat Icelanders or tourists? I decided to play it safe for the sake of my stomach and eat safe foods such as rye bread, some Skyr which most tourists think is yogurt, and some Kakósúpa, cocoa soup. Plus, a hot dog from the famous Pyslur hot dog stand. I didn't want to eat something weird and have to spend one minute longer in the plane's bathroom, if Jaws didn't agree with me.

Japan: Grasshoppers

Who would have thought that these long-legged insects are a delicacy and a source of protein? Not me!

A World of Salads

You could arrive somewhere blindfolded and within a few mouthfuls of salad, know exactly where you are.

Bulgaria (Shopska Salad)

Tomatoes, peppers, onions, cucumbers, and Sirene cheese.
Salad dressing: Red wine vinegar and sunflower oil.

France (Niçoise Salad)

Tomatoes, tuna, potatoes, lettuce, French green beans, onions, hard-boiled eggs, black olives, and anchovies.
Salad dressing: Red wine vinegar and olive oil.

Greece (Greek Salad)

Tomatoes, feta cheese, cucumbers, onions, and Kalamata olives.
Salad dressing: Olive oil and oregano.

(Crete-Greece) Cretan Dakos Salad

Barley rusks, feta cheese or mizithra, capers, oregano, Kalamata olives, onions, and tomatoes.
Salad dressing: Olive oil and red wine vinegar.

Italy (**Caprese Salad**)

Tomatoes, basil, and mozzarella.

Salad dressing: Olive oil.

Mexico (**Caesar Salad**)

Romaine lettuce, croutons, and anchovies.
Salad dressing: Garlic, black pepper, salt, olive oil,
lemon juice, Dijon mustard, mayonnaise, white wine
vinegar, Parmigiano-Reggiano, egg yolk, and
Worcestershire sauce.

Note: There are many variations of Caesar Salad
dressing.

USA (Cobb Salad)

Tomatoes, lettuce, chicken breast (skinless and not
fried), hard-boiled eggs, bacon, avocado, blue cheese,
or Roquefort cheese.

Salad dressing: Vinaigrette dressing.

USA (Waldorf Salad)

Celery, walnuts, apples, and grapes.

Salad dressing: Mayonnaise and lemon juice.

Christmas Foods & Christmas Markets

Festive times call for festive foods that are only served or available during the holidays which makes them very special.

Christmas Foods

Finland-The Finns like to drink a cup of Glögi, a spicy red mulled wine. Kinkku or baked ham is a popular dinner choice. Sweets such as Piparkakut (gingerbread cookies) and Joulutorttu, star shaped pastries dusted with powdered sugar and filled with prune jam can be found all over.

France-Bûche de Noël might look like a yule log with all its decorative accents, but this chocolate cake roll with chocolate whipped cream is meant to be eaten.

Germany-The Germans enjoy Lebkuchen cookies which have a spicy gingerbread and honey flavor. The cookies can be round, star or heart shaped, etc. Another German Christmas cookie is the Zimtstern which is a gingerbread like cinnamon, sugar, and almond star shaped cookie.

Italy-The Italians feast on fish and pasta on Christmas Eve. The region/area in Italy dictates how many dishes are served such as 7 or 13 with 7 symbolizing the seven sacraments. Eels are popular in Southern

Italy. Panettone is a traditional Italian sweet dessert bread. While Ricciarelli, chewy almond cookies, might have hailed from Siena, they can be found outside of Tuscany.

Malta-The Maltese satisfy their sweet tooths with Qaghaq tal-ghasel (honey rings) treacle filled pastries that have no honey in them. They also indulge in Maltese Christmas logs, almond biscuits, and almond cake. And they drink Imbuljuta Tal-Qastan which is a hot drink with a cinnamon, cocoa, chocolate, orange, and chestnut flavor.

Poland-Carp, stuffed pierogi and mushroom soup are usually served for the holiday dinner followed by sweets such as poppy seed roll, almond roll, fruitcake, and cheesecake (Sernik), etc.

UK-Mince pies, Christmas cake & Christmas pudding.

Christmas Markets
England-Birmingham and London
Estonia-Tallinn (Town Hall Square)
Finland-Helsinki (Senate Square)
France-Toulouse (Place du Capitole)
Germany-Frankfurt
USA-NYC and Philly

DIY COOKING

COOKBOOKS

AUSTRALIAN

Australian Food by Bill Granger

Bill'S Sydney Food by Bill Granger

BRITISH/ENGLISH

Gordon Ramsay's Great British Pub Food by
Gordon Ramsay and Mark Sargeant

Jamie Oliver's Great Britain: 130 Of My Favorite
British Recipes, From Comfort Food To New
Classics

Marco Pierre White's Great British Feast: Over 100
Great British Recipes From a Great British Chef

Sunday Roast
(The Complete Guide To Cooking And Carving) by
Clarissa Dickson Wright and Johnny Scott

The Hairy Bikers' British Classics by Si King & Dave
Myers

Tom Kerridge's Proper Pub Food by Tom Kerridge

CARIBBEAN
BAJAN (Barbados)

barbadosbooks.com

JAMAICAN

Levi Roots' Reggae Cookbook by Levi Roots

DANISH

Copenhagen Food: Stories, traditions, and recipes by Trine Hahnemann

EUROPEAN

(Eurotunnel Le Shuttle) The Europhile's Cookbook (A celebration of European food with over 60 recipes)

FRENCH

Lulu's Provençal Table by Richard Olney (Foreward by Alice Waters)

Mastering the Art of French Cooking by Simone Beck, Louisette Bertholle, and Julia Child

The Little Paris Kitchen-Rachel Khoo

GREEK

Under the Olive Tree: Recipes from My Greek Kitchen by Irini Tzortzoglou

The Real Greek with Tonia Buxton

INDIAN

An Invitation to Indian Cooking by Madhur Jaffrey

Dishoom: From Bombay with Love by Kavi Thakrar, Shamil Thakrar, and Naved Nasir

Fresh India: 130 Quick, Easy and Delicious Vegetarian Recipes for Every Day by Meera Sodha

Madhur Jaffrey's Indian Cookery

Madhur Jaffrey's Instantly Indian Cookbook

The Curry Guy: Recreate Over 100 of the Best British Indian Restaurant Recipes at Home by Dan Toombs

ITALIAN

A Table in Venice: Recipes from my home by
Skye McAlpine

Pizza: History, Recipes, Stories, People, Places, Love
(A Book by Pizza Pilgrims) by James Elliot and
Thom Elliot

POLPO: A Venetian Cookbook (Of Sorts) by
Russell Norman

JAPANESE

Harumi's Japanese Kitchen by Harumi Kurihara

Harumi's Japanese Home Cooking by
Harumi Kurihara

MALAYSIAN

Malaysia: Recipes from a Family Kitchen by Ping
Coombes

MEXICAN

Mexican Food Made Simple by Thomasina Miers

The Cuisines of Mexico by Diana Kennedy

SPANISH

Rick Stein's Spain: 140 New Recipes Inspired by My Journey Off the Beaten Track by Rick Stein

THAI

Thai in 7: Delicious Thai Recipes in 7 Ingredients or Fewer by Sebby Holmes

VEGGIE & VEGETARIAN

Asian Green: Everyday plant-based recipes inspired by the East by Ching-He Huang

The New Vegetarian Cooking for Everyone by Deborah Madison

WORLD CUISINE

Jack Stein's World on a Plate: Local produce, world flavours, exciting food by Jack Stein

The Around the World Cookbook: Over 350 Authentic Recipes from the World's Best-Loved Cuisines by Linda Fraser

The Roasting Tin Around the World (Global One Dish Dinners) by Rukmini Iyer

COOKING CLASSES & SCHOOLS

LOCALBITES (Cooking Made Easy)
localbites.co
(Online Classes & In Person Classes)

EUROPE
FRANCE
Le Cordon Bleu
cordonbleu.edu
Worldwide campuses.

INDIA
Delhi Magic

NORDICA/SCANDINAVIA
ICELAND
Reykjavík
Salt Eldhús
salteldhus.is
Offers a one-day cooking class.

NORTH AFRICA
MOROCCO
Fez
Café Clock/CLOCK
cafeclock.com

UK
ENGLAND
London (Wembley Park)
Bread Ahead
Restaurant and classroom.

GHI Cookery School

Waitrose & Partners Cookery School
experiences.waitrose.com
Offers virtual/online experiences.
waitrose.com/cookeryschool

USA
Sur La Table
surlatable.com
Offers Online Cooking Classes and In-Store Cooking Classes.
Sur La Table Online Culinary Institute

FOODIE TV COOKING SHOWS

Food Network TV Channel

The Hairy Bikers' Asian Adventure

Hairy Bikers' Best of British
James Martin's Food Map of Britain
The Hairy Bikers' Food Tour of Britain
The Great British Bake Off
The Great British Bake Off: An Extra Slice

Rick Stein's Secret France
The Little Paris Kitchen: Cooking with Rachel Khoo

Jamie Cooks Italy

James Martin's Mediterranean

Rick Stein's Spain

Wonderful World of Cakes
Wonderful World of Chocolate

FOOD PODCASTS:

Life on a Plate (Waitrose & Partners)
Monocle 24: The Menu
Table Manners with Jessie Ware

FOOD & DRINK FUN

MOVIES

WINE MOVIES:

A Good Year (French Wine-Provence)

A Tale of Autumn (Romance)

Bottle Shock (French and Californian wine production and competition.)

Sideways (SO CA Pinot Noir)
(A wannabe writer and his crazy friend on their two-man bachelor wine oriented getaway.)

Sour Grapes

Uncorked
(Father/Son with different food & drink dreams.)

Wine Country
(Chick flick about turning 50 with the girls.)

Wine for the Confused

Year of the Comet (Romance)

FOOD MOVIES:

Babette's Feast (Food & Wine)

Big Night

Burnt

Chef (Food Truck in USA)

Chocolat (Chocolate)

Fried Green Tomatoes

Jiro Dreams of Sushi

Julie & Julia (Julie, a food blogger, and Julia Child)

My Dinner with Andre

No Reservations

Off the Menu (Mexican)

Tampopo (Ramen noodles)

The Founder (McDonald's)

The Hundred-Foot Journey (French & Indian)

The Lunchbox (Indian tiffin lunchbox)

Toast

Waitress (Pies and relationships)

CUTE FOOD MOVIES FOR KIDS:

Chicken Run

Cloudy with a Chance of Meatballs

James and the Giant Peach

Lady and the Tramp

Ratatouille

Willy Wonka & the Chocolate Factory

BOOKS

Eat, Pray, Love: One Woman's Search for Everything Across Italy, India and Indonesia by Elizabeth Gilbert

Garlic and Sapphires by Ruth Reichl

How To Eat by Nigella Lawson

Hungry by Grace Dent

Kitchen Confidential by Anthony Bourdain

Medium Raw by Anthony Bourdain

People Who Love to Eat Are Always the Best People (And Other Wisdom) by Julia Child

Tender at the Bone by Ruth Reichl

EUROPE

FRANCE

Acquired Tastes by Peter Mayle

A Moveable Feast by Ernest Hemingway

French Lessons: Adventures with Knife, Fork, and Corkscrew by Peter Mayle

Lunch in Paris: A Delicious Love Story, with Recipes by Elizabeth Bard

Paris, My Sweet: A Year in the City of Light
(And Dark Chocolate) by Amy Thomas
(NYC references, too.)

Paris Revealed: The Secret Life of a City by Stephen Clarke

ITALY
Bella Tuscany (The Sweet Life in Italy) by Frances Mayes

USA

(The Hamptons)
The House That Ate the Hamptons: A Novel of Lily Pond Lane by James Brady

(Nantucket)
The Blue Bistro by Elin Hilderbrand
The Beach Club by Elin Hilderbrand

(New Orleans)

The Chef (A Very Tasty Thriller) by
James Patterson with Max DiLallo

Tales from Margaritaville by Jimmy Buffett

UK

A Cheesemonger's History of The British Isles by
Ned Palmer

Food in England by Dorothy Hartley

Scoff: A History of Food and Class in Britain by Pen
Vogler

Taste: The Story of Britain Through Its Cooking by
Kate Colquhoun

The Biscuit: The History of a Very British Indulgence
by Lizzie Collingham

The Philosophy of Cheese by Patrick McGuigan

FOOD ACTIVITIES

TOURS & WALKS

EUROPE

CZECH
Prague
Prague Food Tour
prague-food-tour.com

Taste of Prague
tasteofprague.com

GREECE
Thessaloniki
eat & walk
eatandwalk.gr

Urban Adventures-Tastes of Thessaloniki
thessalonikiurbanadventures.com

MALTA
maltauk.com/gastronomytrail

SLOVENIA
Ljubljana
Ljubljana Urban Adventures
ljubljanaurbanadventures.com

Top Ljubljana Foods Tour
Roundabout Travel
travelroundabout.com
travel-slovenia.com

Ljubljananjam Food & Drink Walks
ljubljananjam.si

tasteslovenia.si
slovenia.info

NORDICA/SCANDINAVIA

SWEDEN
Stockholm
foodtoursstockholm.se
Walking food tour.

ICELAND
Reykjavík
The Reykjavík Food Walk
thereykjavíkfoodwalk.com

CHANNEL ISLANDS (GUERNSEY)
visitguernsey.com
Tasty Walks-20 self-guided island walks.

USA

CO
Denver
Delicious Denver Food Tours
deliciousdenverfoodtours.com
Food, cocktails, beer, and wine tours.

Taste of Denver Food Tours
denverfoodtours.com
Walking food tour.

Local Table Tours
localtabletours.com

PA
Philadelphia
Food Tour
tasteofphillyfoodtour.com

SC
Charleston
charlestonculinarytours.com

FOOD FESTIVALS

EATER BEWARE: Please check with the festival's website as some events may be virtual, postponed, or canceled.

ENJOY!

ICELAND
Reykjavík
Reykjavík Food & Fun Festival
foodandfun.is

CHANNEL ISLANDS

GUERNSEY
Guernsey International Food Festival
visitguernsey.com

Tennerfest
tennerfest.com
(October-November)

JERSEY
Eat Jersey Food Festival
jersey.com

EUROPE

FRANCE
Bordeaux
Bordeaux Wine Festival (June)
Bordeaux S.O. Good (November)

UK

ENGLAND
London
Hampton Court Palace Food Festival
hrpfestivals.com

Oxford
Foodies Festival Oxford

Oxfordshire/Cotswolds
The Big Feastival
thebigfeastival.com

USA

CA
Carpinteria
Annual California Avocado Festival (October)
avofest.com

NY
Hudson Valley Restaurant Week
hudsonvalleyrestaurantweek.com

PA
Kennett Square
Mushroom Festival
mushroomfestival.org
(1st Weekend after Labor Day)

Pittsburgh
Picklesburgh- 3-day pickle festival
picklesburgh.com
(Pickle Juice Drinking Contest)

SC
Charleston
Charleston Wine + Food Festival
charlestonwineandfood.com

Lowcountry Oyster Festival (Annual)

FOOD GUIDES

EATER BEWARE:

Places do come and go. Please check open hours before venturing anywhere. Due to world events, some of the listed restaurants might be offering delivery and take-out only instead of dine-in.

ENJOY!

RESTAURANT GUIDES & APPS

AAA

Eater (USA-Atlanta, Austin, Boston, Chicago, Dallas, Denver, Detroit, Las Vegas, Los Angeles, Miami, NY, Philadelphia, Portland, San Francisco, Seattle, and Washington, DC, etc.)
(Montreal, Canada & London, England)
eater.com

Forbes Travel Guide

Michelin Guide
guide.michelin.com

Tatler Address Book for The Best of Everything
(Dine & Imbibe)

The Good Food Guide (Waitrose & Partners)
thegoodfoodguide.co.uk
(UK restaurants)

Where Chefs Eat: A Guide to Chefs' Favorite
Restaurants (Publisher: Phaidon Press Limited)

ZAGAT
zagat.com

MenuPix (USA & Canada)
menupix.com
Restaurant locator and menus.

HappyCow
happycow.net
Find vegan and vegetarian restaurants worldwide
along with reviews.

RESERVATION APPS:

OpenTable

RESY
resy.com

FOOD DELIVERY SERVICES

allmenus.com & Zomato (Menu information)

ASIA
foodpanda (foodpanda.com) (Delivery-12 countries.)
Hungry Now (hungrynow.co.th) (Thailand-Pattaya)

EUROPE
Glovo (glovoapp.com)

UK
Deliveroo (deliveroo.co.uk)
Just Eat (just-eat.co.uk)
Hungry Panda (Chinese food and groceries delivery.)

SUPPER (Delivery from London's best restaurants.)
supper.london

Uber Eats

USA
Caviar (trycaviar.com)
DoorDash
Grubhub, Seamless, and Yelp
goPuff
Postmates
Uber Eats

FOOD HALLS & FOOD MARKETS
EUROPE

AUSTRIA
Vienna
Naschmarkt

FRANCE
Lyon
Les Halles De Lyon-Paul Bocuse
halles-de-lyon-paulbocuse.com

ITALY
Florence
San Lorenzo Market and Mercato Centrale

Venice
Rialto Market

MALTA
Valletta
Is-Suq Tal-Belt
Valletta Food Market
issuqtalbelt.com
Triq il-Merkanti

THE NETHERLANDS
Amsterdam
Foodhallen
foodhallen.nl
Bellamyplein 51

The Food Department
thefooddepartment.nl
Nieuwezijds Voorburgwal 182, Magna Plaza

POLAND
Warsaw
Hala Koszyki
koszyki.com

PORTUGAL
Lisbon
Time Out Markets
timeoutmarket.com

SPAIN
Barcelona
Mercado de La Boqueria
boqueria.barcelona
La Rambla 91

Mercat de Sant Antoni
mercatdesantantoni.com

Bilbao
Mercado de La Ribera

Madrid
Mercado de San Miguel
mercadodesanmiguel.es

NORDICA/SCANDINAVIA

ICELAND
Reykjavík
Hlemmur Mathöll (Hlemmur Food Hall)
hlemmurmatholl.is
Laugavegur 107

Grandi Food Hall & Fish Market
grandimatholl.is

FINLAND
Helsinki
Hietalahti Market Hall
hietalahdenkauppahalli.fi

The Old Market Hall
vanhakauppahalli.fi

UK
ENGLAND
London
Borough Market
boroughmarket.org.uk

Brixton Village & Market Row
(brixtonmarket.net)

Market Halls
markethalls.co.uk
472 Fulham Road (Fulham)
191 Victoria Street (Victoria)
9 Holles Street (West End)

Mercato Metropolitano
mercatometropolitano.co.uk
42 Newington Causeway

Manchester
Mackie Mayor

USA
Time Out Markets
timeoutmarket.com
(Boston, Chicago, NYC & Miami)

CA
LA
Grand Central Market
grandcentralmarket.com
317 S. Broadway

Santa Barbara
Santa Barbara Public Market
sbpublicmarket.com

San Francisco
Ferry Building Marketplace/Farmers Market
ferrybuildingmarketplace.com

CO
Denver
The Denver Central Market (RiNo area)
denvercentralmarket.com

Avanti F & B
avantifandb.com

The Source Hotel & Market Hall (RiNo area)

LA
New Orleans
The French Market

MI
Detroit
Eastern Market
easternmarket.org

NY
NYC
Chelsea Market-75 9th Avenue & 15-16th Streets
Near the elevated free High Line public park/walk.

OH
Cleveland (Ohio City)
West Side Market
westsidemarket.org
ohiocity.org
100+ year old food market.

PA
Philadelphia
Reading Terminal Market
ReadingTerminalMarket.org
12th & Arch Streets (Close to Convention Center.)

The Bourse
theboursephilly.com

SC
Charleston
Workshop
workshopcharleston.com
1503 King Street

UT
Near Park City (Holladay, UT)
SOHO FOOD PARK
sohofoodpark.com
Check website for days/hours open.

WA
Seattle
Pike Place Market
pikeplacemarket.org

FARMERS' MARKETS
EUROPE

BULGARIA
Sofia
Rimskata Stena-Local Farmers & Healthy
(Saturday morning)

ESTONIA
The Onion Route area for onions.

SLOVENIA
Ljubljana
Central Market at Vodnikov Trg.
Tip: Check out the Indoor Market, Outdoor Market, and the Open Kitchen (March-Oct). (**lpt.si/trznice**)

UK
ENGLAND
London
City & Country Farmers' Markets
weareccfm.com

London Farmers' Markets
lfm.org.uk
London has more than 15 farmers' markets.

USA

CA
Costa Mesa
SOCO Farmers' Market
farmermark.com/soco
Saturdays 9 AM-2 PM

Santa Barbara
sbfarmersmarket.org
Santa Barbara has a few area markets from Tues-Sun.

Santa Monica
Downtown Market-Wed & Sat mornings.
2nd & 3rd Streets and Arizona Avenue.

MI
Detroit
Eastern Market
easternmarket.org
Year-Round Saturday Market (6 AM-4 PM)

NY
NYC
Union Square Greenmarket
grownyc.org
Union Square West & East 17th Street
(Open Mon, Wed, Fri & Sat)

PA
Ardmore (Philadelphia Main Line)
Ardmore Farmers Market (Upscale & Indoors)
120 Coulter Avenue

UT
Park City
Park City Farmers Market
ParkCityFarmersMarket.com

Park Silly Sunday Market *(On Main Street)*
parksillysundaymarket.com

SLC
Downtown Farmers Market
SLCFarmersMarket.org

GOURMET GROCERY STORES

UK
ENGLAND
London
Harrods Food Hall *(Knightsbridge)*

Selfridges London Foodhall *(400 Oxford Street)*

Partridges *(Chelsea)*

Waitrose & Partners Grocery Store (UK Chain)

USA
UT
Park City
Park City Provisions By Riverhorse

USA Gourmet Grocery Store Chains
(CA) Bristol Farms (Upscale)
(CT & NYC) Citarella (Upscale)
(NYC) Gourmet Garage
Trader Joe's (East & West Coast USA)
Whole Foods (East & West Coast USA)
World Market
(NYC) Zabar's

International Gourmet Chains
Whole Foods (Canada and UK)

ASIAN

INTERNATIONAL CHAINS
Wagamama (Japanese cuisine & noodles)
YO! (yosushi.com)

(UK & USA)
itsu (Sushi, noodles, soups & Asian cuisine)

ASIA
JAPAN
Kyoto
Nishiki Market
kyoto-nishiki.or.jp

Kyoto
Ichiwa

Tokyo (Ginza)
Shiseido The Store/Shiseido Parlour Shop
parlour.shiseido.co.jp

SINGAPORE
Lau Pa Sat Hawker Centre
visitsingapore.com
Eat Hainanese chicken rice here.

EUROPE

FRANCE
Paris
Yen
yen-paris.fr
22 Rue Saint-Benoît (6e)
Freshly made soba noodles.

UK

ENGLAND
London
Bang Bang Oriental Foodhall *(Colindale)*
bangbangoriental.com

Bone Daddies (Ramen noodle chain)
bonedaddies.com

East Street Restaurant
eaststreetrestaurant.com
A mix of Asian cuisine in a casual & hip setting at
reasonable prices.

Japan Centre
japancentre.com
(Leicester Square, White City, and Stratford)

Master Wei Xi'An
masterwei.co.uk

Tonkotsu (Ramen noodle chain)
tonkotsu.co.uk

NORDICA/SCANDINAVIA
FINLAND
Helsinki
Fat Ramen
Lönnrotinkatu 34

USA

NY
NYC
Yama (Sushi & sashimi)

PA
Pittsburgh
Everyday Noodles (everydaynoodles.net)
Ki Ramen (kiramenpgh.com)
Noodlehead (noodleheadpgh.com)

Down South
Georgia, North Carolina & South Carolina
CO (Southeast Asian Cuisine Chain) **eatatco.com**

AVOCADO

Avocado Festival:
CA
Carpinteria
Annual California Avocado Festival
avofest.com
(October event)

AUSTRALIA
Gold Coast (Burleigh / Burleigh Heads)
Commune
1844 Gold Coast Highway

UK

ENGLAND
London
Avobar
avobar.co.uk
24 Henrietta Street (Covent Garden)

BREAD

Princi ® (Asia, Italy, UK & USA)

UK
ENGLAND
London
GAIL's Bakery
gailsbread.co.uk

Bread Ahead Bakery
breadahead.com

USA
NY
NYC
Sullivan Street Bakery
sullivanstreetbakery.com

PA
Philadelphia
Le Bus Bakery
lebusbakery.com

Metropolitan Bakery
metropolitanbakery.com

Pittsburgh
Five Points Artisan Bakeshop

BURGERS

ASIA
Hong Kong
BLT Burger

AUSTRALIA
Betty's Burgers & Concrete Co.
bettysburgers.com.au

EUROPE
FRANCE
Paris
Big Fernand (Chain)

Lyon
burger & WINE
burger-wine.com

GREECE
Athens
The Burger Joint
burgerjoint.gr
1 Ninfon Square (Glyfada)

NORDICA/SCANDINAVIA
FINLAND
Helsinki
Friends & Brgrs
Mikonkatu 8

Naughty BRGR
naughtybrgr.com
Lönnrotinkatu 13

SOUTH AMERICA
ARGENTINA
Buenos Aires
PÉREZ-H
perez-h.com

USA
MI
Detroit
Basement Burger Bar
basementburgerbar.com
1326 Brush Street

PA
Pittsburgh
BRGR
brgrpgh.com
2 locations & a food truck.

BURGH'ERS BREWING
burgherspgh.com
3601 Butler Street

UK BURGER CHAINS
Byron Proper Hamburgers
Dirty Burger
Gourmet Burger Kitchen (GBK)
Honest Burgers
MEATliquor
Patty & Bun
Tommi's Burger Joint

USA BURGER CHAINS
In-N-Out Burger
TK Burgers (Orange County-Southern CA)
Umami Burger

INTERNATIONAL BURGER CHAINS
Black Tap Craft Burgers & Beer
Five Guys Burgers and Fries
Shake Shack
Smashburger

CAKES

SRI LANKA
Colombo
Mitsi's Delicacies

UK
ENGLAND
London
Cutter & Squidge
cutterandsquidge.com
20 Brewer Street (SOHO)

THE HUMMINGBIRD BAKERY (Chain)
hummingbirdbakery.com

USA
CA & TX
SusieCakes
susiecakes.com

SC
Charleston
Carmella's Cafe & Dessert Bar
carmellasdessertbar.com

CANDY

NORDICA/SCANDINAVIA

FINLAND
Helsinki
Behnford's
behnfords.fi
Bulevardi 22
Sells American and British candy.

UK

ENGLAND
London
Candy Town
candytown.co.uk
19 Chalk Farm Road (Camden)

North Yorkshire (Yorkshire Dales)
The Oldest Sweet Shop
oldestsweetshop.co.uk
39 High Street, Pateley Bridge

USA

DYLAN'S CANDY BAR (USA Chain)
dylanscandybar.com

IT'SUGAR (USA Chain)
itsugar.com

OH
Cleveland
B.A. Sweetie Candy CO.
sweetiescandy.com
6770 Brookpark Road (At Ridge Road)

IL
Chicago
Candyality
candyality.com

CARIBBEAN

CARIBBEAN FOOD TOURS:

Bahamas (Nassau)-Tru Bahamian Food Tours
Barbados (Bridgetown)-Lickrish Food Tours
Barbados-lickdebowlfoodtours.com
Jamaica-Jamaica Culinary Tours

BARBADOS (visitbarbados.org)
Brown Sugar Restaurant

Oistins' Friday Night Fish Fry
Flying fish and tuna cooked while you wait. Music.

ST. LUCIA (stlucia.org)
Castries Market-An old Caribbean market with
local crafts, Lucian foods, spices, and fruits &
veggies. Saturday is the best day to visit.

Jump Up (Street Party)-Gros Islet-Friday Nights.
Seafood Fridays-Anse La Raye-Every Friday.

W2E Now (Where 2 Eat app)
Tropical Traveller magazine

ENGLAND
London
Head down south to Brixton and Pop Brixton for
Caribbean and Jamaican fare.

CHEESE

UK
ENGLAND
London
La Fromagerie
lafromagerie.co.uk
(Online Store and Stores in Bloomsbury, Highbury &
Marylebone)

Neal's Yard Dairy
nealsyarddairy.co.uk

Paxton & Whitfield
paxtonandwhitfield.co.uk
93 Jermyn Street

Pick & Cheese (Seven Dials Market)
(Pick cheese from a conveyor belt.)

The Cheese Bar (Camden Market)

The Cheese Truck (Maltby Street Market)

USA
NY
NYC
Murray's Cheese
254 Bleecker Street

CUPCAKES

EUROPE

POLAND
Kraków
Cupcake Corner
cupcakecorner.pl

UK
ENGLAND
London
Peggy Porschen *(Chelsea & Belgravia locations)*
peggyporschen.com

Primrose Bakery *(Primrose Hill)*
primrose-bakery.co.uk
(Cocktail Cupcakes)

USA
CA
LAX Airport-Tom Bradley International Terminal

Santa Monica
Vanilla Bake Shop
vanillabakeshop.com

NJ
Chester
Sweet Spot Bake Shoppe
sweetspotbakeshoppe.com
57 Main Street

NY
NYC
Billy's Bakery (Chain)
billysbakerynyc.com

Butter Lane Cupcakes
butterlane.com

East Coast & West Coast USA
Sprinkles
sprinkles.com
(Some locations have cupcake ATM's.)

INTERNATIONAL CUPCAKE CHAINS
The Hummingbird Bakery (London & Dubai)

Lola's Cupcakes (UK and Japan)
Shops & Collection Lockers

Magnolia Bakery (Asia, USA & UAE)

DOUGHNUTS
INTERNATIONAL CHAIN-Dunkin' Donuts®

UK
ENGLAND
London
Crosstown Doughnuts
crosstowndoughnuts.com

Doughnut Time
doughnuttime.co.uk

USA
IL
Chicago
Stan's Donuts & Coffee (Chain)
stansdonuts.com

Doughnut Vault

NY
NYC
Doughnut Plant (Chain)
doughnutplant.com

PA
Philadelphia
Federal Donuts (Donuts, Coffee & Chicken Chain)

FISH & CHIPS

UK
ENGLAND
London
Poppies Fish & Chips (Chain)
poppiesfishandchips.co.uk

Rock & Sole Plaice
rockandsoleplaice.com (Covent Garden area)

USA
NY
NYC
A Salt & Battery
asaltandbattery.com

PA
Pittsburgh
The Pub Chip Shop

SC
Charleston
Hank's Seafood Restaurant

CARIBBEAN
BARBADOS (visitbarbados.org)
Oistins' Friday Night Fish Fry

FISH MARKETS

ASIA

JAPAN
Tokyo
Toyosu Market

EUROPE

ESTONIA
Tallinn
Kalamaja Fish Market

CENTRAL AMERICA
PANAMA
Panama City
Mercado de Mariscos

USA

CA
San Francisco
Fisherman's Wharf

WA
Seattle
Pike Place Market
pikeplacemarket.org

GREEK

EUROPE

GREECE

GREECE-IS.COM

Kea Island   (Cyclades)
Aristaios Experiential Farm & Store
Learn about bees & honey. Organic and Greek
groceries. Nearby folklore museum.

Naxos
Tzimplakis
Local food from Naxos such as cheese and olive oil.

tyrokomia-naxou.gr
(Athens and Naxos stores)

Thessaloniki
eat & walk
eatandwalk.gr

Urban Adventures-Tastes of Thessaloniki
thessalonikiurbanadventures.com

Titania Bakery

UK
ENGLAND
London
isle of olive-6c Ada Street Hackney (E. London)
Stylish taverna & Greek grocer near Broadway Mkt.

The Real Greek (Chain)
therealgreek.com

USA
IL
Chicago
Visit **Greektown** located around Halsted, Madison,
and Van Buren Streets.

MI
Detroit
Astoria Pastry Shop

NY
NYC
Periyali
35 West 20th Street

Southampton (The Hamptons)
Hamptons Greek Festival & Greek Night Out
(Summer events)

GELATO

Global Gelato
GROM (grom.it)

EUROPE
ITALY
Naples
Mennella ll Gelato

Venice (Venezia)
Gelateria Nico

UK
ENGLAND
London
Gelateria Danieli *(Richmond area)*

Gelupo

Ruby Violet

USA
DC *(Washington)*
Dolci Gelati

PA
Pittsburgh
Mercurio's Artisan Gelato and Neapolitan Pizza

ICE CREAM

EUROPE
FRANCE
Paris
Berthillon (*4th Arrondissement***)**

UK
ENGLAND
London (Chinatown & Kentish Town)
Mamasons Dirty Ice Cream
dirtyicecream.co.uk
Filipino ice cream such as Ube with purple yam.

USA
Salt & Straw *(Chain in CA, FL, OR & WA)*
saltandstraw.com

CA
San Francisco
Mitchell's Ice Cream

NY
NYC
Ample Hills Creamery (Chain)

Big Gay Ice Cream (Chain)

Van Leeuwen Ice Cream (Chain)

OH
Cleveland
Sweet Moses, Soda Fountain & Treat Shop
sweetmosestreats.com

Ohio City
Mason's Creamery (World inspired flavors.)
masonscreamery.com

PA
Philadelphia
The Franklin Fountain
franklinicecream.com

Pittsburgh
Millie's Homemade Ice Cream (Small chain)

Olyphant (Montdale)
Montdale Dairy

Clarks Summit & Scranton
Manning Farm Dairy

UT
Park City
Java Cow Café & Bakery

ITALIAN

UK

ENGLAND
London
Mercato Metropolitano
mercatometropolitano.co.uk
42 Newington Causeway

Lina Stores & Lina Delicatessen
Lina Restaurant

(UK Pasta Boxes Delivery)
Pasta Evangelists
pastaevangelists.com
Order pasta, sauce, and garnish for home cooking.

USA

NY
NYC
Veniero's Pasticceria & Caffe
venierospastry.com
venierosnewyork.com
342 E. 11th Street (Between 1st & 2nd Avenues) (EV)
(Cannoli, Cheesecake, Tiramisu & Italian cookies.)

PA
Ardmore (Main Line Philly-Philly Suburb)
Carlino's
carlinosmarket.com
(Artisan food store with Italian focus.)

Philadelphia
DiBruno Bros.
dibruno.com
(Gourmet market with Italian focus.)

Italian Market
italianmarketphilly.org
South 9th Street (Offers ten blocks of food.)
Near Carpenter Street and Washington Avenue.

INTERNATIONAL ITALIAN CHAINS
EATALY
eataly.com
(Stores & Restaurants in Italy & USA)

ITALIAN CUISINE TOURS
Chicago-Chicago Pizza Tours
Philadelphia-9th Street Italian Market Tour

LITTLE ITALY AREAS (USA)

Baltimore, MD
Boston, MA
Chicago, IL
Cleveland, OH
NY, NY
Philadelphia, PA-South Philly
San Francisco, CA-North Beach

PIZZA

Chicago, IL & Naples, Italy Pizza Tip:
For local sources, please refer to the story,
"Eating Pizza in Chicago, IL & Naples, Italy."

UK
ENGLAND
London
Franco Manca (Chain)
L'Antica Pizzeria Da Michele (*Marylebone & Soho*)
Made of Dough (*Shoreditch & Peckham*)
Pizza East (*Portobello & Shoreditch*)
Pizza Pilgrims (Chain)
Voodoo Ray's (Chain)

USA
NY
NYC
Famous Original Ray's Pizza
Joe's Pizza (joespizzanyc.com)
Lombardi's Pizza
Two Boots (*EV, WV & Williamsburg (Brooklyn)*)

PA
Philadelphia
Pizzeria Vetri (Chain)

POLISH
POLAND

krakow.inyourpocket.com

Kraków
Bezogródek Food Truck Park
Dajwór 21 Food Truck Park
Judah Square Food Truck Park

USA

NY
NYC
Veselka (veselka.com)
144 Second Avenue and 9th Street (East Village)

OH
Cleveland
Tip: Try a Polish Boy kielbasa sandwich fused with French Fries and coleslaw.

PA
Pittsburgh
Pittsburgh Pierogi Truck (**pghpierogitruck.com**)
Pierogies Plus on Island Ave *(In McKees Rocks)*
S & D Polish Deli on Penn Ave
Stuff'd Pierogi Bar

NORDICA/SCANDINAVIA

SWEDISH CUISINE

SWEDEN
visitstockholm.com
Stockholm

Enjoy Fika at Vete-Katten, Grillska Huset,
Vurma, Chokladkoppen, or Drop Coffee Shop

Tössebageriet
tosse.se
Karlavägen 77

UK
ENGLAND
London
ScandiKitchen
scandikitchen.co.uk
61 Great Titchfield Street *(Fitzrovia)*
Pastries & open-faced sandwiches. Mini store sells
black licorice and Swedish food.

USA
NY
NYC
Scandinavia House
scandinaviahouse.org
58 Park Avenue

FINNISH CUISINE

FINLAND
helsinkithisweek.com
Helsinki
Stockmann's Department Store (Basement)

Herkku Food Market

Hakaniemi Market Hall

STREET FOOD MARKETS

UK

ENGLAND

London

Borough Market (Visit Wednesday to Saturday)

Broadway Market (Open Saturday)

Camden Market (Open every day)

Flat Iron Square

Kerb (London markets) (kerbfood.com)

Leather Lane Market

Maltby Street Market (Open Saturday & Sunday)

37 Maltby Street

maltby.st

Old Spitalfields Market

Pop Brixton (popbrixton.org)

Vinegar Yard *(Bermondsey)*

USA

UT

Holladay

SoHo Food Park

sohofoodpark.com

Food trucks May-September (Thursday-Saturday)

VEGGIE

HappyCow
happycow.net
Find vegan and vegetarian restaurants worldwide
along with reviews.

UK
ENGLAND
London
Veggie Pret (Chain)

USA
(Philadelphia, PA & Washington, DC)
Hip City Veg
hipcityveg.com

OR
Portland
Sweetpea Baking Co.

INTERNATIONAL HEALTH FOOD CHAIN
RESTAURANTS
by CHLOE. (UK & USA)
eatbychloe.com

LEON. Naturally Fast Food
(Ireland, Netherlands, Norway, Spain, UK & USA)

UK HEALTH FOOD CHAIN STORES

Holland & Barrett
Planet Organic (Several locations in London.)

USA HEALTHY FOOD GROCERY SHOPPING CHAIN STORES

MOM's Organic Market (DC, MD, NJ, PA & VA)

INTERNATIONAL HEALTHY FOOD GROCERY SHOPPING CHAIN STORES

Whole Foods

CHOCOLATE
RESOURCES GUIDES

CHOCOLATE STUFF

CHOCOLATE BOOKS:
Cocoa: An exploration of chocolate, with recipes by
Sue Quinn

CHOCOLATE TV SHOWS:
Rachel Khoo: A Chocolate Christmas
Wonderful World of Chocolate

CHOCOLATE MOVIES:
Willy Wonka & the Chocolate Factory
Chocolat

CHOCOLATE EVENTS

CARIBBEAN

ST. LUCIA
November-Chocolate Heritage Month

EUROPE

SLOVENIA
Čokoljana
cokoljana.mojacokolada.si

UK

ENGLAND
London
The Chocolate Show London

USA

NY
NYC
NYC Chocolate Show-Salon du Chocolat NY
November event.

CHOCOLATE MUSEUMS
EUROPE

ESTONIA
Tallinn
Chocolala
chocolala.ee
Suur-karja 20
Free museum, café, and shop

GERMANY
Cologne
The Chocolate Museum (Schokoladen Museum)
schokoladenmuseum.de
Am Schokoladenmuseum 1a
(15-minute walk from Cologne Cathedral.)
Paid museum and café.

UK

ENGLAND
London
The Chocolate Museum *(Brixton)*
thechocolatemuseum.co.uk
Open Saturday & Sunday.

York
York's Chocolate Story (Interactive)
yorkschocolatestory.com

USA

Nevada
Henderson
Ethel M Chocolates
ethelm.com
(Self-Guided Viewing Aisle)
2 Cactus Garden Drive

CHOCOLATE RESTAURANTS

INTERNATIONAL
Max Brenner

EUROPE

ESTONIA
Tallinn
Kehrwieder Chocolaterie
kohvik.ee
Saiakang 1
(Truffles)

Chocolala
chocolala.ee
Suur-karja 20
Free museum, café, and shop.

GERMANY
Cologne
Chocolat Grand Café at The Chocolate Museum
(Schokoladen Museum)
schokoladenmuseum.de
Am Schokoladenmuseum 1a
(15-minute walk from Cologne Cathedral.)

MALTA
Valletta
Sunday in Scotland
sundayinscotland.com
173 Triq Santa Lucija Street

NETHERLANDS
Amsterdam
Pompadour Amsterdam
(Chocolaterie Patisserie Tearoom)
pompadour.amsterdam

NORDICA/SCANDINAVIA

FINLAND
Helsinki

CHJOKO
chjoko.com

Fazer Café
fazer.com
(Café and chocolate shop.)

UK

ENGLAND
London
Copperhouse Chocolate
copperhousechocolate.co.uk
1 Chapel Market

USA

OH
Cleveland
The Chocolate Bar
thechocolatebar.com
347 Euclid Ave

CHOCOLATE SHOPS

EUROPE

France
Lyon
Chokola
chocolatier-bouillet.com
Chocolate faucet.

Palomas
palomas1917.com

CHANNEL ISLANDS

GUERNSEY
Ben Le Prevost Chocolatier
benleprevostchocolatier.com
Old quarter in St. Peter Port.

Handmade artisanal infused chocolates with flavours
such as Coffee, Lemon Verbena, Miso, Peach,
Pistachio, and Rosemary.

Ben is a true chocolatier.
Academy of Chocolate and the International
Chocolate Awards (European and British)

UK

Hotel Chocolat (Chain)
hotelchocolat.com
Hotel Chocolat has cafés, stores, and restaurants in the UK.

USA

See's Candies
chocolateshops.sees.com

CA
Santa Barbara **(santabarbaraca.com)**
Chocolate Maya
15 W. Gutierrez Street
Chocolates and Hot Chocolate.

NY
Brooklyn
Jacques Torres
mrchocolate.com
66 Water Street (First location)
Manhattan-A few locations.

PA
Hershey
Hershey's

SC
Charleston
Christophe Artisan Chocolatier-Pâtissier
The French Chocolate Cafe
christophechocolatier.com
90 Society Street

WA
Seattle
Theo Factory & Flagship Store
theochocolate.com
3400 Phinney Ave N

HOT CHOCOLATE VENUES

EUROPE

SPAIN
Madrid
Maestro Churrero Chocolateria
Chocolate topped churros. Hot chocolate.

UK

Hotel Chocolat (Chain)
hotelchocolat.com

USA

NY
NYC
Mariebelle
mariebelle.com
484 Broome Street (SoHo)

Serendipity 3
serendipitybrands.com
225 East 60th Street
(Frrrozen hot chocolate)

COCKTAIL STUFF

DIY COCKTAILS

COCKTAIL BOOKS:

Bartenders' Manual: And A Guide for Hotels and
Restaurants by Harry Johnson & Thomas Majhen-
Editor

Behind the Bar: 50 Cocktail Recipes from the
World's Most Iconic Hotels by Alia Akkam

Cocktails & Canapés: How to throw the very best
party, whatever the size by Kathy Kordalis

Cocktails Made Simple: Easy & Delicious Recipes for
the Home Bartender by Amin Benny and Brian
Weber

(Esquire) Drink Like A Man
The Only Cocktail Guide Anyone Really Needs
Introduction by David Granger & Edited by
Ross McCammon and David Wondrich

Fiestas: Tidbits, Margaritas & More
(75 Mexican-Style Cocktails And Appetizers) by
Marcela Valladolid

Gin O'Clock (A Year of Ginspiration)

With Over 70 Delicious Recipes To Guide You
Through The Seasons by A Craft Gin Club Guide

Mixing Cosmopolitans: The Pouring Tales by Daniel
Staub

Noble Rot Book: Wine from Another Galaxy by
Andrew Mark and Dan Keeling

The Art & Craft of Coffee Cocktails: Over 80
Recipes for Mixing Coffee and Liquor by Jason Clark

The Essential Cocktail Book: Classic and Modern
Cocktail Recipes For Every Day incl. Gin, Whisky,
Vodka, Rum and More by Peter A. Morgan

The Fine Art of Mixing Drinks by David A. Embury

The Martini Cocktail: A Meditation on the World's
Greatest Drink, with Recipes by Robert Simonson

The Negroni: Drinking to La Dolce Vita, with
Recipes & Lore by Gary Regan

Vogue Cocktails
(Classic Drinks From The Golden Age Of Cocktails)
by Henry McNulty

DRINKS GUIDES

BARS & PUBS GUIDES

Note: There are too many bars & pubs in the world to list here. That's a separate bar book! Please refer to the following guides and apps for bars and events:

worldsbestbars.com
A handy website for discovering bars in about 200 cities!

UK
The Good Pub Guide
thegoodpubguide.co.uk

drinkaware.co.uk for drinking safely.

London Cocktail Week

ICELAND
Reykjavík Grapevine Happy Hour app-Appy Hour (grapevine.is)

USA
BARCADE *(CA, CT, NY, NJ & PA)*
barcade.com
Bar + video games/arcade = BARCADE.

Florida (floridabeachbar.com)

BEER TOURS

EUROPE

IRELAND
Dublin
GUINNESS Storehouse
guinness-storehouse.com
St. James's Gate

POLAND
Tychy (80 minutes by car from Krakow)
Tyskie Brewery
browarytyskie.pl

USA

CO
Denver
Denver Beer Trail
denv.co/denverbeertrail

Fort Collins
Anheuser-Busch Brewery Tour
budweisertours.com

Golden
Coors Brewery Tour
coorsbrewerytour.com

NY
Brooklyn
Brooklyn Brewery
brooklynbrewery.com
79 N 11th Street

OH
Cleveland
Great Lakes Brewing Company
greatlakesbrewing.com

DRINK MUSEUMS

MIDDLE EAST

ARMENIA
Yerevan
ARARAT Brandy

Ararat Museum (**araratbrandy.com**) and Yerevan Brandy Company are located near the Hrazdan River. Tours are offered in Armenian, English, French, German, and Russian. It's best to book in advance.

NORDICA/SCANDINAVIA

SWEDEN
Stockholm
Spritmuseum and Absolut Vodka
(**spritmuseum.se**)

WINE MUSEUMS

EUROPE

FRANCE
Bordeaux
Musée Du Vin Et Du Négoce
museeduvinbordeaux.com

La Cité du Vin
laciteduvin.com

Paris
Musée du Vin de Paris
museeduvinparis.com
5 Square Charles Dickens (16th Arr.)
Might be closed on Sundays & Mondays.

GERMANY
Deidesheim
Museum Fur Weinkultur Museum

GREECE
Thessaloniki
Gerovassiliou Wine Museum
gerovassiliou.gr
Closed on Tuesdays.

PORTUGAL
(Porto) **Museu do Vinho do Porto**

WINE TOURS & TASTINGS

EUROPE

FRANCE
Bordeaux
Rustic Vines Wine & Bike Tours
rusticvinestours.com

MALTA
maltauk.com/bartrail

GREECE
Santorini
Santorini Wine Trails
santoriniwinetrails.gr

Santorini Wine Adventure
winetoursantorini.com

Santorini Wine Tour
santoriniwinetour.com

SLOVENIA
Ljubljana
Ljubljana Wine Experience
visitljubljana.com

USA

CA
Santa Barbara
Santa Barbara Urban Wine Trail
urbanwinetrailsb.com

Sonoma

winecountrywalkingtours.com

sonomacounty.com

Sonoma County Grape Camp
sonomagrapecamp.com

HOT DRINKS
GUIDES

COFFEE SHOPS

AUSTRALIA
Gold Coast
Commune
1844 Gold Coast Hwy.
Burleigh Heads (Queensland)
Open every day from 6 AM-3 PM.
Carefully crafted Flat Whites and coffee drinks in a
carefree not far from the beach relaxed café.

ASIA

MALAYSIA
Kuala Lumpur
LOKL COFFEE CO.
loklcoffee.com
30 Jalan Tun H.S. Lee

EUROPE

AUSTRIA
Vienna
Café Museum
cafemuseum.at

Café Drechsler

CROATIA
Dubrovnik
Caffe Bar Art
The Scoop: Casual indoor & outdoor café with some seats made from old bathtubs.

FRANCE
Bordeaux
L'Alchimiste Café Boutique
12 Rue de la Vieille Tour

SLOVENIA
Ljubljana
Riverside Promenade area has a good selection of cafes.

NORDICA/SCANDINAVIA

SWEDEN
Stockholm
Drop Coffee Roasters
dropcoffee.com or dropcoffee.se

Johan & Nyström
johanochnystrom.se
A few locations in Stockholm and Sweden.

UK

ENGLAND

London

GRIND

grind.co.uk (Cool coffee chain.)

Kaffeine

The Attendant (Chain)
the-attendant.com

Workshop Coffee

London Coffee Events:
The London Coffee Festival (Spring)

USA

MI

Detroit

Astro Coffee
astrodetroit.com

Lucky Detroit Finely Crafted Coffee & Espresso
(Corktown area)
luckydetroit.com

Stella Good Coffee
Fisher Building
3011 W. Grand Blvd.

Urban Bean Co.
urbanbeanco.com
200 Grand River Ave
Accepts bitcoin.

NY
NYC
Irving Farm coffee (Chain)

The Grey Dog (Chain)

Starbucks Reserve Roastery
starbucksreserve.com
61 9th Ave (15th Street)

NEVADA
Las Vegas
PublicUs
1126 Fremont Street
(Fremont East District-Downtown)

OH

Cleveland

Erie Island Coffee Company
erieislandcoffee.com
2057 E. 4th Street

Rising Star Coffee Roasters
risingstarcoffee.com
Small coffee chain.

Six Shooter Coffee
15613 Waterloo Road

OR

Portland

Coava on Grand
coavacoffee.com
A few locations in Portland.

Heart
heartroasters.com

Stumptown Coffee Roasters *(CA, NY & OR)*

PA

Pittsburgh

Big Dog Coffee

Commonplace Coffee Co. *(Small coffee chain.)*

Espresso A Mano
espressoamano.com
La Prima Espresso Co.
laprima.com

SC
Charleston
Kudu Coffee & Craft Beer

UT
Park City
Park City Coffee Roaster
pcroaster.com

Pink Elephant Coffee Shop
509 Main Street

VA
Alexandria
Misha's
mishascoffee.com
917 King Street

GLOBAL COFFEE EVENTS:
globalcoffeefestival.com

TEA TASTING TOURS & MUSEUMS

SRI LANKA
Nuwara Eliya
Pedro Estate

UK
ENGLAND
London
Twinings Tea Shop & Museum
twinings.co.uk
216 Strand
(Tube: Temple)

Tiny museum with a small store that sells loose and teabag teas. A small tasting of chosen teas is available.

Cornwall (Truro)
Tregothnan Tea Estate
tregothnan.co.uk

USA
SC
Charleston area (Wadmalaw Island)
Charleston Tea Plantation

WHERE TO TAKE TEA

EUROPE

FRANCE
Lille
MÉERT
meert.fr

UK
ENGLAND
London
Most luxury and boutique hotels offer lovely afternoon teas.
Refer to London Planner for venues.
londonplanner.com

Dedham
Essex Rose Tea Room

Tiptree
Wilkin & Sons Ltd. of Tiptree Jams and Conserves, Tearooms and Museum
tiptree.com.

York
Bettys Café Tea Rooms
bettys.co.uk

COFFEE, TEA & BOOKS CAFÉS

EUROPE

FRANCE
Paris
Merci (Used Book Café)
111 boulevard Beaumarchais *(3rd Arr.)*
Look for the cute little red car out front.

Shakespeare and Company Café
shakespeareandcompany.com
37 Rue de la Bûcherie
Close to Notre Dame Cathedral.

POLAND
Kraków
Massolit Books & Café
massolit.com

UK
ENGLAND
London
London Review Bookshop

London (Green Park Area)
Maison Assouline
A beautiful selection of books.

USA

CA
San Francisco and Corte Madera (Bay Area)
Book Passage
bookpassage.com
A café and vast travel literature section are present in the Corte Madera store.

DC
Washington
Kramers *(Dupont Circle area)*

NY
NYC
Shakespeare & Co.
939 Lexington Avenue *(Upper East Side)*

PA
Philadelphia
Shakespeare & Co.
1632 Walnut Street

GETTING THERE

TRAVEL RESOURCES

ASIA

HONG KONG
(Hong Kong) discoverhongkong.com

JAPAN
(Japan) jnto.go.jp
(Japan) japan.travel
(Tokyo) gotokyo.org

SINGAPORE
(Singapore) visitsingapore.com

THAILAND
(Thailand) tourismthailand.org

INDIA
(India) indiatouristoffice.org

SRI LANKA
(Sri Lanka) srilanka.travel

AUSTRALIA
(Sydney & Melbourne) imfree.com.au

CARIBBEAN

(Barbados) visitbarbados.org

(Jamaica) visitjamaica.com

(Saint Lucia) stlucia.org

EUROPE

AUSTRIA

(Vienna) wien.info

BULGARIA

(Bansko) banskoblog.com

CROATIA

(Croatia) Croatia.hr

CZECH REPUBLIC

(Czech Republic) visitczechrepublic.com

ESTONIA

(Tallinn) tallinn.inyourpocket.com

FRANCE

(France) france.fr

GERMANY

(Frankfurt) frankfurt-tourismus.de

GREECE
(Greece) greece-is.com

IRELAND
(Dublin) dodublin.ie

ITALY
(Milan) welcometomilano.it

MALTA
(Malta) visitmalta.com

POLAND
(Kraków) visitkrakow.com

PORTUGAL
(Porto) visitporto.travel

SLOVENIA
(Ljubljana) visitljubljana.com

SPAIN
(Spain) spain.info
(Madrid) esmadrid.com

NORDICA & SCANDINAVIA

FINLAND
(Finland) visitfinland.com
(Helsinki) helsinkithisweek.com

ICELAND
(Iceland) guidetoiceland.is
(Reykjavík) visitreykjavik.is

SWEDEN
(Stockholm) visitstockholm.com
(Stockholm) stockholminfo.com

CENTRAL & SOUTH AMERICA

ARGENTINA
(Buenos Aires) turismo.buenosaires.gob.ar

PANAMA
(Panama) visitpanama.com

UK

ENGLAND
(Birmingham) visitbirmingham.com
(Liverpool) visitliverpool.com
(London) cityoflondonguides.com
(London) londonplanner.com
(London) thelondonvisitors.co.uk
(Manchester) visitmanchester.com
(Oxford) oxfordcity.co.uk

USA

VisitTheUSA.com
wheretraveler.com

CA
(Santa Barbara) santabarbaraca.com

FL
(Miami) miamiandbeaches.com
(Florida Keys) visitflorida.com/florida-keys

MA
(Martha's Vineyard) mvol.com
(Martha's Vineyard) mvy.com

MI
(Michigan) michigan.org
(Detroit) visitdetroit.com

NJ
(Atlantic City) atlanticcitynj.com
(Princeton) visitprinceton.org

NY
(NY) iloveny.com
(NYC) cityguideny.com
(NYC) nycgo.com

OH
(Cleveland) thisiscleveland.com

OR
(Portland) travelportland.com

PA
(Philadelphia) visitphilly.com

SC
(Charleston) explorecharleston.com

Washington, DC
washington.org

NAVIGATION

TRANSIT APPS & WEBSITES:

Citymapper

Google Maps

rome2rio.com
Type in your destination and find out estimated costs
& trip length via plane, bus, train, or car.

thetrainline.com
(Trains & Buses in the UK & Europe.)

Waze

CAR SERVICE/RIDES:

Lyft (lyft.com)
Uber (uber.com)

CAR SHARES:

Zipcar (zipcar.com)

PUBLIC BIKE SHARE SOURCES

Mobike-mobike.com

EUROPE

BULGARIA
Sofia (sofiabike.com)

CZECH REPUBLIC
Karlovy Vary (cd.cz)

FRANCE
Paris-Vélib' (velib-metropole.fr)
Bordeaux-Vcub (infotbm.com)

ITALY
Lake Como (Bike&CO)
Milan (bikemi.com)

GREECE
Thessaloniki (THESSBIKE)

NORDICA/SCANDINAVIA

FINLAND
Helsinki (hsl.fi)

UK

ENGLAND
Liverpool-City Bike (citybikeliverpool.co.uk)
London-Santander Cycles
(santandercycleslondon.co.uk)

USA

East Coast
Chicago-Divvy Bikes (divvybikes.com)
Detroit-(mogodetroit.org)
Miami-Citi Bikes (citibikemiami.com)
NYC-Citi Bikes (citibikenyc.com)
Philadelphia-Indego (rideindego.com)
Washington, DC-(capitalbikeshare.com)

West Coast
San Francisco-Ford GoBike (fordgobike.com)

BURNING CALORIES

WALKS

SOUTH AMERICA

ARGENTINA
Buenos Aires
buenosairesfreewalks.com
10:30 AM-(Recoleta Tour)

3 PM-City Center at The Front Gate of the National Congress.

UK

ENGLAND
London
Low Line Walk (Bankside area)

Start at the Shard building near London Bridge to Southwark and pass through Borough area. You can stop off at Borough Market or Flat Iron Square for food & drink. Perhaps see some art at Tate Modern?

BEE Midtown
bee-midtown.com
Free guided walks in Bloomsbury, Clerkenwell, Farringdon, Holborn, and ST. Giles.

USA

CO
Denver
Denver Free Walking Tours
denverfreewalkingtours.com

NY
NYC
The High Line (thehighline.org)
A walk on the elevated High Line is an ideal way of exercising and sightseeing at the same time. Closes at sunset. You can start in the Meatpacking District (MPD) near the Whitney Museum of American Art at Gansevoort & Washington Streets and end up anywhere before or at 34th Street near Macy's dept. store in Herald Square. There are 10 access points along the walk.

The Brooklyn Bridge
Walk, bike, ferry, or subway between Manhattan and Brooklyn.

NJ
Atlantic City
Atlantic City Boardwalk
4+ miles long.

RUNNING APP: rungoapp.com
(USA Cities, London & Paris, etc.)

STEPS

ASIA
Hong Kong (Lantau Island)
Big Buddha & 268 steps.

MIDDLE EAST
ARMENIA
Yerevan
The 572 Steps of the Cascade Complex

USA
NY
NYC
The Vessel at Hudson Yards

UK
ENGLAND
London
The Monument (themonument.org.uk).
Climb the 311 steps of the Monument.

Tube Stations-Climb up or down the straight or windy staircases or long escalators in the Big Smoke.

CONTINUING FUN WITH THE AUTHOR

FREE CONTINUE THE FUN READER & FOLLOWER BENEFITS:

FREE STUFF LIKE ANSWER BASIC ? BUT STILL VERY HELPFUL TRAVEL ADVICE.

NEW BOOK NEWS & WEBSITE UPDATES

SURPRISE!!
TWO CONTESTS PER YEAR
ON JUNE 1 & DEC 1 (SURPRISE PRIZES) FOR SIGNED UP CONTINUE THE FUN FRIENDS.

FOR FREE SIGN UP:
Send e-mail to:
havefun@foodietravelnearandfaratravelbook.com

No personal details are required-Only a valid e-mail is required to continue the fun!
In subject body of e-mail put your location of residence such as New York City or Oxford, England.
Winners and subscribers will be contacted via their e-mail address.
foodietravelnearandfaratravelbook.com

NOTES OF GRATITUDE

I'm very appreciative of my family and friends. Thanks for listening to me go on and on over the years about how I wanted to write travel books to help guide and inspire others.

I'm most grateful to my kind mother & father who love me unconditionally and listen/listened to my writing & travel dreams. The only condition for any travel was a phone call home every so often to assure them of my safety since postcards might take some time to reach them. A small price to pay for freedom and for seeing this wonderful world which I love so much! Unfortunately, my father, a pilot as a young man, will never read any of my books since he passed away a few years ago while I was in the friendly skies on the way to see him.

"Thanks, Bubba, for being curious about the world, too. I know it was hard for you to do while you were busy working and raising a large family."

Philly Super Dave, you're a friend to the end! And a good software editor. Thanks for understanding all the technical challenges I faced with getting this book out there. And for all your help across the pond. Thanks for still being my friend after it was all done!

Thank you, Joana Nanci, for your graphic design help, talent, devotion, and all around kindness.

Janice and Tiny, thank you for your kindness and encouragement. Many special thanks to Milly J, Pam, TPG, BW, Maryanne, Lo, Sheila, Stephen, Oswaldo, Nicholas, Jim, PA aka TT, Tikki, G, CPG, Chuck, Mini, Li, Tippy, BP, and C & A.

There are so many people who were kind to me on the open road whose names I don't know. Please know how much I appreciated any & all little random acts of kindness that mean so much to a weary traveler. Travel is full of trials and tribulations! A shared ride, a gift of a piece of fruit, a bottle of water, or a seat in a crowded lobby, mean more than you might ever know. Thank you for making those moments easier. Thank you!!

And to some people who I will never meet such as Anthony Bourdain, Peter Mayle, Amelia Earhart, and Jan Morris. Thanks for making such important contributions to food and travel!

An extra special thanks to very kind and supportive contemporaries, friends & acquaintances: Eric, Mike, Jennifer & The Lee Family, Yannis, Tony, Anthony, Lor, Joanne, Eric, David, Jill, Tami, Jim, Jane, Richard, Lisa & Lee, Emma, H & J Down Under,

Nancy, Barbara, Aunt Mary, Susie, Aunt Ginny, my Grandparents, All my Cousins, Aunts & Uncles, Robyn & Michelle, Mary Ann, Ann Marie, Beth, R & C, Jim & Sheila, Joyce, Alma & Jim, Arvid & Pam, Nelson, and Barry M & his parents.

A special thanks to Patrick Luteran of gingerspizen for his continuing moral support and professional graphic design work & consulting.

Colleen, thanks for your sisterly friendship and for all the beautiful writing journals you've gifted to me over the years. To Michelle & Jill at Smythson of Bond Street, thanks for selling me many lovely blue page travel journals & notebooks.

Eileen, at the East Hampton Library, thanks for teaching such a wonderful creative writing course so many years ago. And to the staff at the East Hampton Library, thanks for always being so nice and helpful.

To my writer friends (Matthew, Marty, Silje, BV, Ron, Louisa, Paula, and Guorún from Iceland).

Catherine, thanks for backpacking with me through Europe 31 years ago. Edouard & Oshen, thank you for your Parisian kindness.

JSH, thanks for the book, "Round the World with the Empress of Britain," you gave me 30+ years ago. It's been my constant travel buddy. Thanks to Julie, Tommy & Megan, for the Dr. Seuss book, "Oh, the Places You'll Go!," for my college graduation.

DKLI & LD, thanks for the referral and for your friendship. Jeff and Beth, you both are inspirations. All I did was write a book. You learned to talk again after major illnesses.

To all my old co-workers at Broadway & Prince in NYC. I really enjoyed working with such an internationally diverse group of people. I learned a lot about global cuisine at lunchtime when lunchboxes were opened. You inspired me to travel, so that I could eat the same food. (Franco, Greg, JL, H, Ben, Wei, Victor, Jim, Philippe, Fred, NM, Ellen, Deborah, Amy, Gil, LD, Clyde, Stacey, BD, and Aakar, etc.). And to Hiuwai for always seeing life with a unique eye.

For those who have shared their love of country with me: Ray & Wendy (Australia), Olivier (France), Annie (India), Chris, Jamie & Kevin (Ireland), Claire, Lisa, Al & Ramona (Italy), Yuko (Japan), Mr. & Mrs. P & family (Sri Lanka), Patricia (South America), Stephan (Switzerland), Tulin, W & L, Jen, Mark A, Daniel, AR, Ag & Debbie, and Mr. Smith (My high school History & Spanish Teacher). Thank you!!

ABOUT THE AUTHOR

C. R. Luteran is based in the UK where she is a freelance travel writer in the fields of travel, tourism, and Food & Beverage. She holds a Marketing & Business degree from the University of Scranton and a Professional Certificate in Marketing & Advertising from New York University's School of Continuing Education. She attended Book Passage's Travel Writers & Photographers Conference.

While NYC was home for 17 years where she worked in Silicon Alley & the garment district, she still considers Philadelphia her home away from home.

Caron's true passion, purpose, and love in life has always been for travel both near & far. She has been fortunate to have explored 50 countries, 15 islands, and 32 USA states.

The next place is either somewhere new or someplace old with new eyes. It's hard to pick a favorite place as travel experiences are correlated to the seasons and to your state of mind. However, there are 1 or 2 places she won't go back to. And there are 1 or 2 places that she will go to again and again, if possible.

HAVE FUN!!

CPSIA information can be obtained
at www.ICGtesting.com
Printed in the USA
LVHW040005300421
686058LV00019B/1482